Cathy Hawkins

Cartwheels on the Faultline

Cartwheels on the Faultline

Works by Twenty-seven Sonoma County Women

Collected by Barbara L. Baer & Maureen Jennings

Floreant Press
Forestville, California

Floreant Press
6195 Anderson Road
Forestville, California 95436

Printed in the USA by Floreant Press
10 9 8 7 6 5 4 3 2
First Edition
2nd Printing

Cartwheels on the faultline: works by twenty-seven Sonoma County women: collected by Barbara L. Baer & Maureen Jennings.
p. cm.
Preassigned LCCN: 95-61967
ISBN 0-9649497-0-9

1. Literature—Women authors. 2. Women—Sonoma County (Calif.)—Literary collections. I. Baer, Barbara L., ed. II. Jennings, Maureen, ed.

PN6069.W65C37 1996 818.54
QBI95-20631

Acknowledgements
Cover painting by Marylu Downing.
Cover design by William Kinnear.
Illustrations for "Ravens" and "Ducks" by Peggy Marrs.
Illustrations, "Krishna Flossing" and "Reclining Woman" by Boschka Layton.
All other original art by Marylu Downing.
Permission to reprint work by Boschka Layton from *The Prodigal Sun:* "Guardian Angel," "Twenty-four Hour Performance," "Is There Hope For The Future Cry the Loud Bells of Palsy," "Wind Chimes, Ivan," "Afternoon In the Sun," courtesy Mosaic Press/ Valley Editions, Box 1032, Oakville, Ontario, L6J 5E9, Canada (ISBN 0-88962-184-5 paper; ISBN 0-88962-189-6 cloth).
"Beginning" by Elizabeth Herron appeared in *Wild Duck Review,* 1995.

Floreant Press

Cartwheels on the Faultline

Table of Contents

Introduction

Our book began as a question to myself. I was alone at my desk feeling bored by my own writing. I'd been working at it for thirty years. What was dulling my voice now? Who and what prevented me from writing to my heart's content? I knew the phrase "heart's content" meant something but I didn't know what. I decided to invite women writers I knew in Sonoma County, and ask them.

Twenty-two women filled both sides of a banquet table at the Union Hotel in Occidental, an old place that specializes in all-you-can-eat Italian dinners. After the food and wine, I asked my friends if they were writing what they most wanted to write. No, came voices up and down the table. Why? Because editors' judgments and the shadows of rejection hang over us, they said. What if we weren't going to be judged and rejected? I asked. We would write with no apologies, no regrets, came the answer.

Before the supper ended, our book was born. We invoked as our guiding spirit a wonderful woman named Boschka Layton who had lived until her death in a cabin above the Russian River. In her sixties, she was writing novels, stories, poems; she also painted and sculpted, travelled on no money, slept wherever she landed, and sustained many of us with her creativity and her fierce independence. She was scared and brave, romantic and irreverent. She'd had Bell's Palsy for a long time. She wrote about how people stared, and she painted her own weeping eye and skewed face. She dared to offend, yet was vulnerable and always kind. That night, we left the hotel in the darkness with her in our minds.

Over the winter we met in a house beneath redwoods that seemed entirely made of light. We ate loaves of bread and soup and greens that appeared on the sideboard; no matter how much we ate, there was always more. We decided we didn't want a theme. We'd throw our nets out to sea and trust the catch that came in.

In the spring when it was warmer, we sat in the sun on a deck around the house. All one morning, a hawk stayed on a pole as we read to each other about losing our mothers; about men, envy, and midlife relationships out of synch; about the amusing, the gross, even the aesthetic use of garbage. We read what we'd never said to anyone.

Around July, there came time for pruning. We'd listened and commented on each other's work in small groups, but as my one-year deadline to finish our book neared, the thorns came out on the roses. When a writer told me, "Without this chance, I wouldn't have written my story," I was thrilled, but with an editor's pencil in hand, I couldn't read every word as sacred. By pulling tight on one thread, was I undoing the delicate weave of a story or essay? Some writers were fragile to my criticism, yet everyone went back again and again to rewrite.

Now that we had content, the problem was our title.

Writing to Our Heart's Content seemed too soft, too fuzzy, for twenty-seven pieces that stayed close to the bone.

Boschka's spirit had been present at the outset, and now when we needed her again, inspiration for our title came from her writing and the shifting shelf of land where we live in northern California. We are in earthquake country, atop fractures and fissures of large and small faults. Only a few years ago, the ground opened in western Sonoma County and a crevasse split a farming valley in two. Boschka's lines on the death of a friend—"Your long gray-flannelled legs/ turn breathless cartwheels in the sand"—came together with our geography as *Cartwheels on the Faultline.* The title expressed Boschka's and our own acrobatics on the edge of the unknown.

I've been rewarded by every writer whose work is in these pages. The book's completion has brought me solace for the loss of my mother Carolyn, my brother Ted, and Boschka Layton, that tattered monarch in her cape of green and orange, who lived voraciously, with no apologies, no regrets. "I lean into blackberry," she wrote,

> pull hot clusters
> from the vine
> I should save them for supper
> instead I
> eat
> every
> one

—Barbara L. Baer, Forestville, September 1995

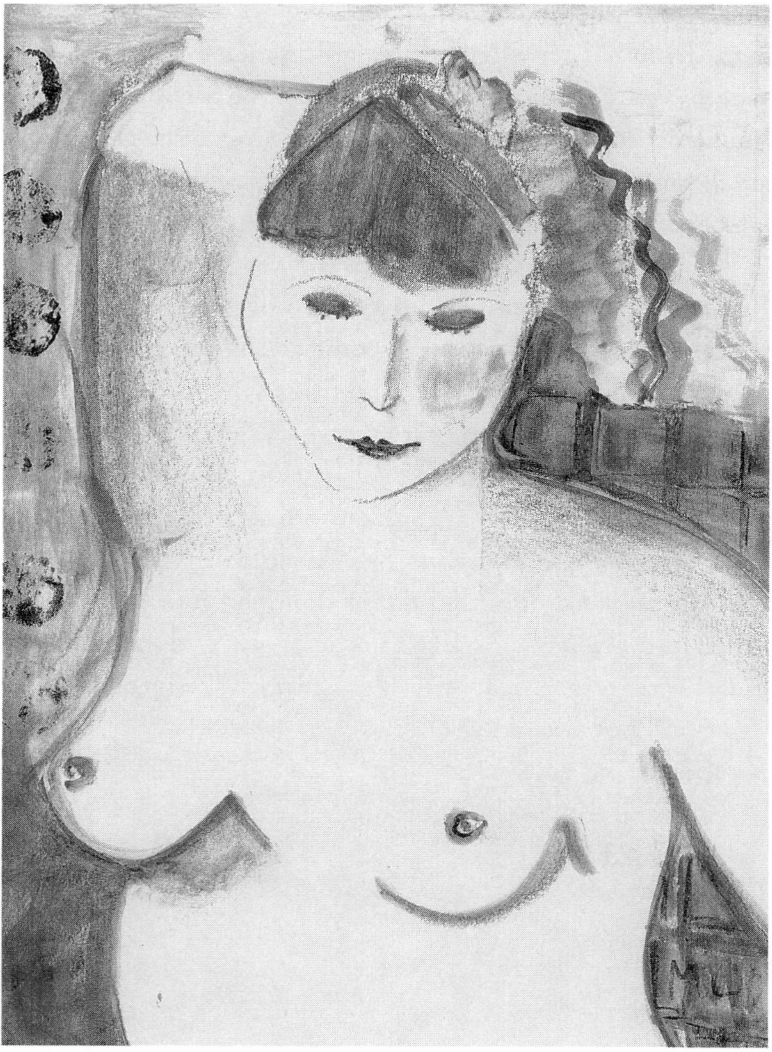

Overexposure

Marianne Ware

The shop was out on the fringes of the business district, less than half a block before commerce ended and the East End residences began. Today, Marsha is trying to remember precisely what it looked like, as if outside appearances, had she truly noticed them, might have warned her of what was about to happen to her there. She's decided that the place had some kind of draped or pinned curtain across the bottom of the window. The top part was so dingy she couldn't have looked inside unless she'd pressed her nose to the glass and cupped her fingers around her eyes to blot out the light.

I think there were old-fashioned cameras on tripods behind the curtain. I could just see the tops of them, sort of blurry-like, when I walked toward the door.

Suddenly, Marsha feels certain of these details, as she ruminates over the events of that day five years before.

I wanted to give Leroy a picture, so he'd never forget he was the first one who . . .

Phillips' Photography, the gold-etched sign informed her.

No, Sullivan's Stills, that seems more like it.

The issue, of course, is not really the name of the establishment or the proprietor. The significant point is that she went there willingly, clutching a month's worth of babysitting money, hoping to be revealed by the camera as cute, or maybe even pretty (since beautiful had never, ever, been possible). What she'd longed for was an image of herself that would linger in the beholder's eye.

The tinkling of the bell attached to the shop's inside door frame once again resonates as Marsha, a twenty-year-old, overweight housewife and new mother, nurses her baby and dissects these memories for the first time in a long while.

It was late summer, 1953, and she and her parents were preparing to leave Long Branch, Long Island, for a new life in southern California. Her father, Mr. Out-of-Work Wanderlust, had set his sights on the West Coast with its warm-all-year weather, less demanding employers and "relatives who'll put us up for as long as we like." Marsha's mother had been snuffling and sighing for days and days now, as she gave notice at the phone company, began sorting their clothes, called about shutting off the utilities, and cleaned up the rented bungalow they'd called home for one entire year.

At this moment, Marsha remembers adoring Long Branch, its long sweep of a sugary-sanded beachfront, its razzle-dazzle of a boardwalk in the summertime, the Lido Theatre with its plush loge-section make-out seats where she'd first been kissed and felt up by Leroy.

Why did they take me away from there, the only place that felt good to me, the only school I ever liked?

How can the move still upset her from a 3,000-mile, half-decade distance? And why has she forgotten the snotty schoolmates who teased her in the girls' locker room during gym class about her two-changes-of-clothes, holes-in-the-bottom-of-her-shoes wardrobe, and her shabby West End address? And Leroy, well, wasn't he third-rate, a user, and obviously happy as hell Marsha would soon be out of his hair? Getting her cherry had been ridiculously easy, and the way she'd hung on him all summer must have been a colossal pain.

Marsha has no insight into the true facts of the situation. Her focus is the shop's entrance, the antique cameras near the window, and then, her first glimpse of Mr. Phillips (or Sullivan?) wiping his hands on a blue (no brown) bibbed apron. But now she can't look at him, that grinning, fortyish photographer, beckoning her to step forward into the cool near-darkness of the shop. Marsha has become ravenous. Breaking the suction of her baby's mouth on her nipple, she deposits Lily in the playpen, then bolts for the kitchen door.

Four years later, our heroine, now twenty-four, is deeply depressed and much, much fatter. Her preschool-age daughter, Lily, is consistently pressed into service as her nurturer, holding Mommy's head in her tiny lap while Marsha cries. She has no idea what is bothering her, why she hates her existence, her own body, even, at times, her seemingly committed husband. Dale confounds her by sticking with the marriage, no matter her emotional problems and grotesque proportions. Her heart nearly stopped the day she found that girlie magazine way, way back on his side of the closet. Flipping the pages to see who was there, what they looked like, left her shaking. She's had to forgive Dale for hiding it, because he swore the women meant nothing to him, that he just wanted her to do it with, if only she'd let him.

It is eleven in the morning, and Marsha, on the couch, has just awakened from a dream where she watched her husband making love to someone who looked just like that Turner girl Leroy went out with before they left Long Branch. It had to be the very same day she'd gone to have her picture taken, after she'd had breakfast with Leroy and he'd promised to be faithful forever. Marsha has never been able to separate ego-engendered fiction from reality. Actually, she hasn't thought about any of this for ages. She wants it all to go away again, but the images keep coming. Now the photographer speaks to her.

"Miss Harwood? Yes, we do have an appointment." He is staring at her, licking his . . .

It was so dark and cool in there; I could hardly see him.

Once again he puts both hands on her shoulders, draws her forward. She seems to have missed part of what he said to her.

"What?" She verbalizes the memory.

"Take your top off and put this around you."

It's nine years after the fact, but she shudders.

How could I have done it so easily, even if what he said sounded logical?

"You don't want to seem ordinary in that plain old blouse thing. I'll drape the velvet so you look like a movie star, like you're out on a date to the Brown Derby."

"Where's that?" Marsha hears herself asking.

"Hollywood, of course," he answers.

"We're moving out west next Friday. My dad has family in Los Angeles; we're going to live with them 'til

Mom starts working."

"Interesting," says Phillips (or Sullivan). "Now go get ready for your sitting."

Twenty-four-year-old Marsha refuses to remember anything further. She gets up from the couch, motions to her daughter to turn off the TV and says, "Let's go for ice cream." Fifteen-year-old Marsha is thus freeze-framed, thwarted in her willingness to follow orders. But maybe she does follow them, over and over again, in some dark, synaptic corner.

Thirty-two-year-old Marsha has had six years of therapy, some of it helpful, some of it tedious. Fifteen-year-old Marsha is still in limbo, while her eighteen-month, three-, nine- and twelve-year-old selves have been much revitalized. Each has her own story. Marsha has come to know them, realize they are shards, fragments of her psyche's broken pottery, that some pieces do fit together, while some remain stubbornly jagged and isolated. She is still fat and married, though somewhat more responsive to her husband, pleased, at least, to be pleasing him, though her own body's needs are foreign to her.

Today, as she walked down Norwalk Boulevard past the newsstand next to the drugstore, she became agitated, went back to the car, and drove home again. Girlie magazines unnerve her.

What if someone read one and saw a person he actually knew there?

Marsha, though older and considerably sharper, still believes, on some deep level, that the women in those magazines look like females are supposed to.

Then how could I be in one?

It's not the first time she's asked herself that question.

But it's seventeen years. He must have destroyed them, the negatives. Hell, he probably thought they were ugly, and never even used them.

At long last, Marsha is back in the shop again, in its tiny dressing room, clutching over her bare breasts, the dusty alien hunk of material Mr. What's-His-Name has just given her.

"Hurry, Miss, I've got more appointments later."

She is freezing there in the semi-darkness, wishing she were anywhere else, even in California without Leroy.

"Come out, dear. You certainly should be ready."

Now she sees herself stepping from behind the partition, taking slow, creak-the-floor steps toward the back-of-the-store divider, from where the man is speaking to her.

"Ah, good, good," he says when he sees her. "Come, sit here on the stool while I prepare the camera."

Marsha's older and younger selves shiver in unison.

What the hell could I have been thinking? Was it some kind of trance, or was I just plain stupid and gullible? But how could I have known what he was up to? It's normal for girls, females, to be draped for professional photos. Even today, everyone knows that. Only why did it have to go further? Was it my fault? Did I ask for it?

Marsha has only recently learned about the women's movement, what it says about men who manipulate. What she's heard both frightens and intrigues her. Unfortunately, at this moment, she is making no connections.

"Ohhh, my dear, you have such beautiful skin tone." Thirty-two-year-old Marsha remembers the precise words he said to her. "You glow; you actually glow," he tells her.

Was that spittle in the corner of his mouth?

Notice how she distracts herself with a basically insignificant detail. Fortunately, the memory is relentless.

"Here, let me adjust the drape for you." The cloth dips lower and lower. Sullivan/Phillips' hands tremble as he fastens the corners of the velvet under her arms at the waistline. Her shoulders are pinioned, strait-jacketed under the velvet.

What did he pin it with, I wonder? Oh hell, does it really matter?

"So you're moving to Hollywood?"

"Well, somewhere around there. My dad has an aunt and some cousins."

"What will you do when you get there?"

"School, I guess."

"College?"

She blushes. "No. I'm still a sophomore."

"No one could guess it. You look at least eighteen, the best age for a girl. Hey, I've got a brother in Los Angeles; he's also a photographer, in advertising. He'd really like you, I mean as a model."

"Me? A model?" The word now, as then, is incomprehensible. But to thirty-two-year-old Marsha it's a giveaway.

That son of a bitch!

At last she can label him.

God, I was so stupid, stupid!

Oh, oh, she's absorbed all blame again, and now she's

up and off for some bites of sweet refrigerated oblivion.

Marsha's daughter has just celebrated her fifteenth birthday. She is twenty years younger than her mother. They have been arguing. Marsha despises Hank Appleton, Lily's boyfriend. She thinks he's a snake, who's out to get what he wants and then too bad for Lily.

"I know his kind," Marsha rasps at her daughter.

"You don't know anything," comes the answer. "Guys were big pricks back in the fifties."

"How can you say that? Your dad was one of them." Her daughter is quiet for a moment. Marsha wonders, for the zillionth time, how she'd managed to avoid a lifetime of Leroys and hook up with Lily's father.

Did I really deserve him? Was it fate that made us leave the Downey Theatre at precisely the same moment, even before the film was over?

"Look," she continues, "I made stupid mistakes, got hurt. I just want you to be happy." Marsha almost said "safe," a word she knows drives Lily crazy. "Gullible" is her own trigger. Despite her mother's caution, Lily has trounced out of the room, leaving Marsha to ponder the depths of her coffee mug.

There, up through the blackness, Leroy emerges. She reaches for the creamer.

He told me about that Taylor bitch in Neeland's Cafe and Coffee Shop. Wow! Where in the hell did that name come from?

Now she remembers the details correctly. It had been weeks since she'd seen him. Then she phoned and begged him to meet her, even though he said he'd have only a few minutes before he was due for work at his uncle's Texaco. She said she was busy too and had an appointment with the photographer.

So their first date wasn't that day. He'd already been seeing her.

Over the years Leroy speaks to her; she can't turn off the audio. "Look, it's over! Jean and I are . . . oh shit, you're not gonna start your damned bawling. That's it. I'm leaving!"

Marsha switches to fast-forward. It's probably okay because she's just faced what she needed to from this sequence, so its power to educate is over. Now she's doing double time in her head up the street to Phillips' and Sullivan's Photography Emporium. Flash! And she's inside, pulling her blouse over her shoulders, then, half a second later, perched on top of the stool as Mr. P/S continues.

"My brother does all the photography for the Montgomery Ward catalogues. Have you seen them?"

"Uh huh," she lies, falling easily into responding as he wants her to. Thirty-four-year-old Marsha startles herself with this recognition. If only she could speak for the girl she was, sneer at the *son-of-a-bitch,* challenge his *bullshit*.

"Did you know all the models' clothing is painted on by artists after the pictures are taken? My brother poses, uh, photographs them, you know in the . . . "

"No . . . ?"

Tell the bastard you know what he's up to. Tell him, TELL HIM!

"What do you mean?" Marsha wants to throttle her fifteen-year-old self for asking another noose-tightening question.

"All models pose in the nude. It's a rule of the business."

Young Marsha doesn't even notice what he's doing now, moving her arms from across her chest to grip the rear of the stool so her head is thrown back and her chest thrust forward. Now he adjusts the drape again. Older Marsha is outraged.

Kick the fucker in the groin; do it!

But of course, that isn't possible. The man is now behind his camera, bright green cloth draped over his *rotten-assed, lying cranium.*

"But how could they stand to?"

He pops his head out from under the covering and stares at her. "Oh, it's old hat to the photographer, just a job; we don't even notice."

"But what about the girls; aren't they embarrassed?"

"Not real models. They're proud of themselves, happy to be making good money and knowing they're attractive and . . . Yes, you certainly are model material. I've never seen more beautiful skin tone. My brother would put you before his camera in a minute. You know, you can get a work permit at sixteen. I'd be happy to give you a recommendation and send him some photos."

"But these are for my boyfriend, so he remembers me."

"I could take other ones, today even. Just a few more shots. Yes, yes, that's lovely, now smile for the birdie."

Marsha sits mesmerized over her coffee cup. The scenario she's immersed in is fascinating and horrifying. She's wholly into it, not even reaching for a cookie.

Now she's fast-forwarding. The draped session is over. Mr. Sneaky/Peaky is maneuvering, cajoling.

"I'll take the shots for free and airmail them to Bernie in the morning, along with a letter of introduction. Look, here's his card. You can call him when you get there. Nobody else will see them. And you'll be on your way to a career like every girl dreams of."

Older Marsha is squirming.

How could I know he was full of it? It was 1953. I was so brainwashed, needy. So what if I wasn't a virgin? I was still mostly innocent. Nobody'd taught me about phony flattery, or how to deny a man what he . . .

Now comes a kaleidoscope of images. The drape is gone from her shoulders, her half-slip, her—even her panties. One must forgive Marsha for leaping over the step-by-steps. What's important is her focus. She has never been as brave before. Shush, he's speaking.

"Your skin, it actually glows, really, I mean it. Here now, up on the platform. Yes, yes, on your knees, hands in front like you're about to take off crawling. Ahhh, Bernie will love this."

But I was so modest. Leroy never really saw me. In gym I'd dress and undress under my slip and stand behind the locker door. How could I let him convince me? People could say I actually wanted him to . . . NO, DAMMIT NO! He was paunchy and balding. I never let him touch me . . . except for the poses. I'm sure I didn't want him to. I couldn't wait to get out of there. But then why did I feel so unworthy? I don't want to remember this. It's so ugly, so awful.

Marsha upsets her coffee cup. She is weeping, weeping. Soon she will be at the cookies, nearly choking as she chomps them. No matter, she won't forget what she's learned here, though she'll need more time to assimilate it.

Forty-some-year-old Marsha is considerably thinner.

She has a reasonably good relationship with her daughter, who has married a decent man like her father. One cannot say Marsha now adores her body, but at least she accepts it. Nowadays, it responds normally, something her husband appreciates. Of course, she still longs for irrefutable proof that Mr. Sleezarian-Prickowsky was a heinous villain, that her fifteen-year-old self was entirely innocent. After all, she never went back, even for the original photos she'd come for, never called him or contacted his brother in Hollywood. (Actually the card said Inglewood.) And hadn't she paid and paid for her sin by maiming her body, denying the love of her husband and enduring that anguished preoccupation with *Hustler* and *Playboy*?

Fifty-some-year-old Marsha is still married to Dale and definitely functional. Does this mean we have come to the proverbial happy ending? Well, not precisely. Marsha returns, occasionally, to the end of the summer of 1953 in Long Branch. She still doesn't know if the photographer was evil incarnate or if she was, somehow, complicitous. Despite all her insights she has no definitive answers. What matters is that she can live with it, precisely as it seems to have happened, exactly as she pictures it.

Work It, Girlfriend

Robin Beeman

"You're just here for the moral support," Ashley says, watching me. "I drove it last night from the rental place and I can do it."

I'm standing in the humid sunshine of an Ohio July morning staring at the behemoth of a moving van and questioning my own judgement. Parked behind the van is the apple-red BMW, my twenty-something daughter's delight that we'll be towing from Cincinnati to California. This all began when my daughter stated she was going to drive back to California by herself. "You can't do that. It just isn't safe," I'd heard myself say. "I'll fly out and drive back with you."

"Only if you really want to, Mom," she'd said.

"I really want to," I'd said. "It will be an adventure."

I bought my plane ticket and worked on convincing myself that everything would be all right, reminding myself of how many times I'd seen just such combos rolling insouciantly along one of our nation's highways. I was getting stodgy and this would shake up my life. It would be a chance for us to spend some time together.

I climb inside. It has air-conditioning, a radio, power steering, automatic transmission—everything, it seems, for people like us who've never gone to trucking school.

Since the rental company does not put the car on the tow rig, we call AAA. The young man they send tells us he's only just started this job. Our first decision is whether to put the front wheels or the back wheels on the rig. He says the front but the car has an automatic transmission and its owner's manual says it should go on backwards. It's clear he's not sure. We agonize and decide to go with the owner's manual. He shrugs and secures the back wheels with some flimsy-looking fabric straps. He hooks two chains onto eyes under the car, leaving the extra length to drag along the ground. Then he drives away.

A man from the apartments comes out and notices that the hitch holding the trailer onto the truck isn't on all the way. He screws it down more. None of this seems very auspicious. We check the cargo inside the truck and tie things down. Ashley puts her house plants on the front seat of the Beemer so they'll get light as we drive. Finally there's nothing more to do.

With great panache Ashley drives away from the apartment complex where she's lived since her divorce and onto the freeway. Each time an eighteen-wheeler passes our van shudders, sucked toward the larger vehicle. Some sort of vacuum effect, I think, watching Ashley grimace, jaw set and knuckles white as she grips the steering wheel. "You're doing great," I say as we turn onto a cloverleaf and I look back to see the Beemer following rump up, nose down like a dog on a scent being pulled backwards. We high five and chortle.

"Work it, girlfriend," Ashley says, something women say in Cincinnati.

We enter Indiana. Lush fields of corn, farmhouses and barns flow by. Rivers spill over their banks. This is the wettest summer on record in the Midwest and cumulus clouds edge up the horizon.

Our first road test comes when I have to pee. Ashley turns wide and glides smoothly under a gas station awning—backing is impossible with the tow rig. I run in and use the bathroom. In the truck again I see a big red notice on the dashboard. WARNING: 11' 0" CLEARANCE. MOST TRUCK RENTAL ACCIDENTS RESULT FROM DRIVING UNDER LOW BRIDGES, SERVICE STATION CANOPIES, ETC.

"Did you think about clearance?" I ask. She shakes her head.

Our next test comes when we need fuel. We're talking fuel, not gas. Diesel. If all those really big trucks have made it, we can too. We pull under the awning of a truck stop. So far so good. In the glove compartment we find an extensive manual on the sound system but only a tiny brochure on the truck and no information on a fuel tank. We walk around the truck, realizing we're being watched by the real truckers. Finally we decide that the ugly black drum hidden under the box of the truck must be it. A screw top with a sign saying DIESEL FUEL ONLY confirms this. As Ashley squats with the hose on the glowing asphalt, I clean the windshield.

"The one thing the rental people stressed was checking the oil," Ashley says when we're done. Fine. We've both put oil in cars. We walk to the front of the truck ready to lift the hood and discover there is no hood. In fact, judging from the flat front of the truck, there doesn't seem to be any engine. We check the brochure again but there's nothing on this situation either. Still, we know there has to be an engine because something did make noise when she turned the key. We locate a diagram inside the driver's door showing that an engine does exist—right under the seat. To get to it we'd have to lift the whole cab of the truck, which seems a little extreme just to put in a quart of oil. Finally, between the cab and the box, I discover a small plastic cup with a cap that says CHECK OIL HERE. Next to it is a dipstick. We check the oil and it seems to be down, very down.

Of course, we get not a clue from the brochure about what sort of oil to put in. A trucker and his son, a young man about Ashley's age who seems to think Ashley in her pink shorts and baggy T-shirt with her Pebbles Flintstone ponytail is pretty cute, are happy to show us what kind of oil they buy. We buy a gallon and fill the plastic cup, wondering if this is indeed the right place to put the oil. Even the trucker and his smitten son aren't 100 percent sure but since they've been so nice we allow them to encourage us.

Back on the road we hear an ominous growling sound right behind us, right where we put the oil. At the very next exit we call the 800 number also pasted on the dashboard. Someone on the other end who doesn't speak much English says not to worry.

"Work it, girlfriend," we say as we plunge into Illinois, through Peoria, then through Galesburg, home of

Carl Sandburg. I imagine some sort of literary experience and ask Ashley to go into town but Galesburg is a depressing place of boarded-up storefronts with bands of sullen teenagers standing on the sidewalks sneering at anyone who makes the mistake of turning off the freeway.

Dusk arrives and I insist that we stop at the very next motel so that we can cross the Mississippi River in full daylight. We pass a farm with a large pond and talk about how nice it would be to have a pond. We talk about bluegill, bass, and crappie. We giggle at the word *crappie* and say it a lot. We talk about relaxing in a motel with a glass of wine. We talk about a party. "Toga. Toga. Toga," we chant. We're getting giddy. The road gets worse. I can feel Ashley growing tired. We drive past signs saying Rock Island, Moline, Chicago, names from Bob Seger songs. No motels appear. A brilliant sunset flares and we try to appreciate it while watching fireflies glittering in the grass. Then we hit a huge hole and a truck tries to run us down.

I advance a theory that, since Davenport is flooded, everyone will have fled to motels and we'll have to sleep in the truck. Suddenly we're on Interstate 80 and crossing the bridge to Iowa. "The Mississippi," I say. Only inches below the bridge the Mississippi stretches, a lake, an ocean, its pewter surface streaked by moonlight and broken by the tops of trees, the roofs of houses.

As we turn into Davenport nothing looks awash and the motels all have *Vacancy* signs. So much for my theory. The motel manager, who wears a turban, scowls when I mention floods and says scornfully, "That is just a few streets down by the river." We walk out into the humid night and buy wine coolers and popcorn and come back to the big cold room to watch Jay Leno, who used to be a lot funnier. We take turns in the shower.

The next morning we see that Iowa, which is supposed to be under water, is only flooded in the logical places. The young man filling our tank lives right on the Buffalo River. "The government gave us some money after the first flood this spring to put in some new flooring and we'd just gotten it in when this came," he says, bemused by it all.

The road narrows to one lane each way as road crews make repairs. It rains. By midday Ashley is frazzled and I suggest a stop. As if by magic, a gleaming white city appears on a hilltop in the middle of a huge cornfield. We pull into the biggest outlet mall ever. Everyone in Iowa who is not bailing is here. We check out what Ralph Lauren, Reebok, and Liz Claiborne have to offer but our only purchases are a couple of Arby's chicken sandwiches.

Near Des Moines we finally see some flooding in low areas. We have a Diet Coke at Burger King because it has the easiest parking lot to get in and out of. Because of our size we park with the truckers. In line a youngish trucker tries to strike up a conversation with Ashley. He asks where she's going.

"Tell me, why are you truck drivers so aggressive?" she asks.

"What do you mean?" he says, trying to look bewildered.

"Don't you ever think about the little guys on the road?"

He can tell already this conversation won't go his way but he still wants to impress her with his wit. "No. I just keep it at 55 and if I hear a crunch I know I hit it." She shakes her head and he goes on talking about jake brakes and honking his horn in tunnels.

More rain. We see a sign pointing to Sioux City. "Where all the lawyers live," says Ashley. By late afternoon we cross the Missouri River and enter Nebraska. It's pouring when we hit Lincoln and locate a motel only to discover everything's full because a Jehovah's Witness convention is in town. Not being on the Witnesses' mailing list we didn't know. We are so daunted the desk clerk takes pity and finds us a room in a place across town.

The next morning I announce I am going to drive. Ashley tells me I don't have to but I can tell that it's time. The rain lets up. We pass a sign directing us to Buffalo Bill's house. This is Willa Cather country. I remember reading "Neighbor Rosicky" in college and being overwhelmed by the grimness of prairie life. We are now paralleling the Oregon Trail. Wind blows the alders along the North Platte River. We're not in a covered wagon but this trip is becoming arduous in its own way. I will put my nervous shoulder to the wheel.

At the next stop, I begin driving. Not bad, I think at first, then whoa. The Beemer is really fishtailing behind us. I wonder if it's shifted on its trailer. I pull into a service station at the next off-ramp and a nice mechanic—everyone is nice in the Midwest—says the Beemer is okay but the straps are loose and the safety chains left dragging are ground all the way through—dear Lord.

We call the rental people and talk this time to a Cajun in Lafayette, Louisiana, who directs us back twenty-six miles to a town where the chains can be welded. We take a side road this time and get right up close to all that corn, passing old houses, silos, all quiet except for insect noises. Red-winged blackbirds and a prairie falcon pattern the air. We arrive at a big barn full of farm vehicles being repaired by a dark-faced Vulcan. Here we find out that the safety chains securing the tow rig to the truck weren't secured. For the first time in years, I think about my guardian angel and say a prayer of thanks.

By dusk we've made it to Ogalala at the hundredth meridian. The air is dry. Even the breeze feels western. We drink wine in the lounge of the motel, a tatty fifties-style room with a huge television and four or five ranchers, compact sun-tanned men in jeans and checkered shirts at the bar. A fey-looking woman comes in to tend bar and flirts with a withered old man, then goes up behind one of the younger men and strokes his shoulders. She wears a loose flowered dress. I'm sure they're lovers.

Ashley and I talk and watch *Seinfeld* on the giant television. The evening takes on a lighter cast as road tensions slip away. I call home and report our progress.

We gas up at a truck stop the next morning surrounded by shirtless, tattooed young men, the kind Brad Pitt must have studied before he tried out for the part in *Thelma and Louise.* Ashley tells me to lock the doors and stay inside while she fills the tank and cleans the windshield. I should be telling her that. She's the one they're eyeing. She's awfully protective of me, which I find very touching. Last night as we were walking to find a place to eat she actually put out her arm to keep me from crossing a street she thought too dangerous.

As she goes in to pay, a commotion breaks out among

several men huddled together. I hear shouting. My heart pounds. The huddle breaks up and the men laugh. My heart is still pounding when I see Ashley come out. So much frightening male energy.

She's at the wheel this morning. Sunflowers line the side roads, windmills, wheat fields—no more corn. The land seems to swell so that when we're on the top of a hill and we look out we see not the horizon but the land dropping away. "The sky just takes over," says Ashley.

We drive through Cheyenne, a drab cluster of buildings around the gilded dome of the capitol. The air smells of gas. Houses are scarcer here and trailers litter the landscape as haphazardly as if dropped from the sky. The Laramie valley is flecked with clouds. After Laramie the rain begins and the wind comes up. The road turns nasty and rutted and the Beemer fishtails madly. Ashley grits her teeth. At Rawlins I take over. The road improves a little, but fighting the wind and the road tires me. At a stop on Elk Mountain, where grey clouds threaten snow, a young man tells us it's been like this all summer. Mines and oil fields pass by. Everything near Rock Springs is a dismal gray. We sleep in Evanston, a collection of buildings huddled around a train track and river.

The Wasatch Mountains with their lush valleys are splendid as we climb to Park City, where a jarring display of condos spills down around yet another outlet mall. The descent to Salt Lake City is steep and terrifying. I smell our brakes all the way down. The Great Salt Lake reeks of decay. It's weird and creepy, this body of dead water. I don't mind leaving it as we zip through the salt flats and enter Nevada where the flashy inducements to investigate the slots actually look welcoming.

Over Nevada the wind forms a glass shelf with fat saucy clouds sitting on it. Trails of snow linger in the crevices of mountains. We're tasting home now, driving through sage and creosote bush and pine and cedar at the higher elevations. There's almost no traffic today and the driving is relatively easy. Ashley talks about doing outdoor things in California, the things she's missed in Ohio. She wants a wind-surfer, a pickup truck.

We stop in Lovelock and drink margaritas at a bar whose surface contains video screens. Ashley speculates on the nature of gamblers. "They're optimists," she says. "They believe they'll win."

"Maybe so," I say, "but the idea of blind luck seems foreign to me. I guess I'm a closet Puritan who believes everything is earned." We watch an old couple sitting in front of a bank of machines, the woman feeding coins, the man studying a board flashing numbers overhead. His face is rapt. A couple of Mexican workers sit beside them. "*Nunca,*" says one of the workers to the other.

At Fernley the next day, a trucker eyes the license plate on Ashley's car and asks why she's leaving beautiful Ohio for awful California. We've noticed that truckers feel obliged to say nasty things about the state. But he can't daunt us. We can almost smell the Pacific by now. Leaving Reno we cheer at the "Entering California" sign as we climb the impossibly beautiful granite Sierras.

The decline into the Sacramento Valley is hairy. After Auburn, cars pour in from every entrance, everyone moving full-throttle. We can feel the tension. I almost long for those empty Nevada highways. If I didn't know that my little home in western Sonoma County was waiting, I might be tempted to turn around. Finally we pull off onto a two-lane road and the bucolic landscape unfolds. Napa. Sonoma. Penngrove. Cotati. Highway 116 appears like the yellow brick road, and Sebastopol—Nuclear Free Zone with Sister Cities in Japan and the Ukraine—is the Emerald City. "Work it, girlfriend," we say and high five as we pull over for the last time.

Four months later I'll get a call at 4:00 a.m. telling me my mother has died. I call Ashley. "I need you to come with me to Louisiana," I tell her. "Moral support."

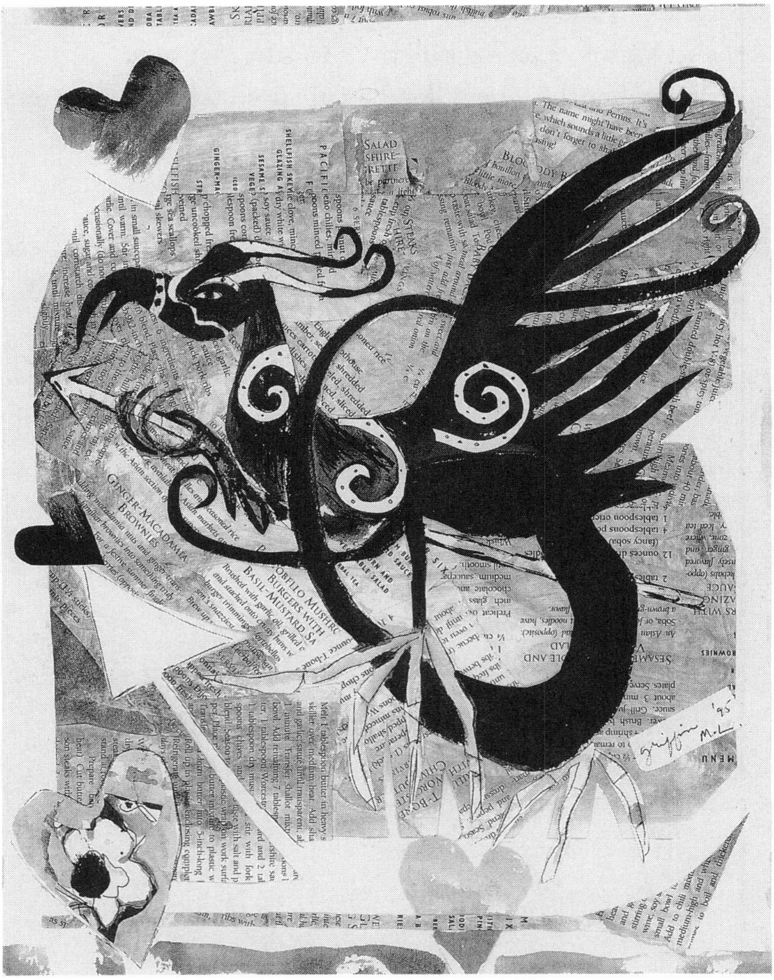

Imaginary Beasts

Maureen Jennings

"My wife wants to kill me. I need more wine." John scraped his empty glass across the patio table's filigreed surface.

"If Nona needed you dead, you'd be in Colma already. You're more likely to die from pneumonia basking on this frigid patio."

Al poured more merlot into their glasses. "What's my sister done now?"

"She wants to put a blast furnace in the backyard. Welding doesn't challenge her anymore; she's decided to start casting her pieces. The landlord won't let her install a furnace at the studio, so she wants the damned thing here." John emptied his wine glass.

"Maybe your wife misses New York in August. Think a furnace would warm it up back here?"

"I suppose burning a garden should produce some heat. She insists the plants won't die."

Al smiled. "The neighbors will think you've got your own little crematorium going here. They'll be watching for milk-carton kids and hoping they can sell video footage to TV."

John hesitated a moment before he laughed. "When I told her I'd rather have a pond, she asked if I wanted toy gondolas to float around on it."

"Still the eternal argument about your Eternal City, John?"

"It's our theme song, the greatest hit on our list of disagreements."

John mocked their marriage's oldest argument in resigned tones. He nurtured fantasies of living in Venice and immersing himself in its subtle colors, reluctantly accepting his native San Francisco as a poor substitute. Nona refused the idea, certain that living in a city so rich in art would paralyze her own creative work. He said "inspire," she said "immobilize."

"Forget Venice. After the gondola crack, Nona said she wanted my face to be the first thing she cast. I didn't know if I was more surprised at her wanting to do representational work or scared to be her first model." John unrolled the sleeves of his shirt and buttoned the cuffs.

"Maybe she'll make us sit out here until we freeze into gargoyles." Al meticulously split the remaining wine between their two glasses, sighing heavily as he placed the empty bottle's neck into the umbrella hole in the center of the table.

As the bottle toppled, John grabbed it and replaced the green neck in the table's center. Palming the bottle's bottom, he pushed down, ignoring the table's rasped complaints and the flecks of white paint chipped loose by the glass.

"She says we have to stay outside till she's finished. She's your sister. You tell me what she's doing."

"I gave up predicting that girl when I reached the age

of reason, long before you abandoned all reason and proposed to her." Al looked over his shoulder as if he expected a waiter to materialize in John and Nona's yard.

Loud thumps and shrill curses sounded from the house. Al and John had almost reached the door when Nona's voice ordered them to stay outside.

John returned to the table, grabbed a pair of clippers from a battered basket, and walked into the garden surrounding the patio. Ignoring the thorns, he cut a large bunch of roses, then roughly deadheaded more blooms into a brown Safeway bag. At Nona's insistence, every rose in the garden was red.

"Two more minutes, gentlemen," Nona called. The french doors opened onto the patio, but the unbleached canvas draperies still blocked any view of the interior. Her grinning head poked out between the drapes like the mistress of ceremonies in a Punch and Judy show.

"I promise it'll be worth the wait." Nona disappeared again, her exit dramatized by the blare of a foghorn.

Al paced around the garden, glowering at the gray fog. "Don't forget you promised to show me your new work tonight."

John grinned. "Plan on a lengthy exhibition of watercolors. I've got three deadlines for illustrations next month. Publishers are in a hellacious rush to put out angel books these days. Too bad your sister won't model for me."

They heard the thud of the front door slamming, then Nona's voice.

"Don't worry, I didn't abandon you two. Look toward the french doors again. Ready?" Without waiting for their reply, Nona slowly drew open the drapes.

"You can come in now."

Nona stood next to her creation, sweaty and excited. She rubbed at her grimy nose and bounced up and down on her toes, semaphoring her excitement.

An enormous sculpture had replaced their round oak dinner table. A huge sheet of beveled glass rested on four contorted copper legs. The spotlights Nona had aimed at her work showed a watery green lurking within the thick glass that glittered above the copper she'd polished to a dull gleam.

John studied the starkly beautiful dining table Nona had created, drawn to the depths of the green glass. He didn't ask what she'd done with the old table.

"Don't you see what the legs are? They're for you, darling."

"It's beautiful, Nona."

"Look at the legs, John."

The forms emerged beneath the glass. Attenuated, abstracted griffins guarded the table, fierce eagles' heads and wings bracing the glass over the lions' heavy hind legs and erect tails. The creatures' predatory beaks extended precisely under each corner of the table.

"I've never seen griffins like these before. You've made them so ferocious. They're almost frightening."

"I worked on them for a long time. They're my last welding project." Nona ran her fingers along the tabletop's thick bevel.

"My plan is that we'll leave the french doors open for hours on end and let the salty air oxidize the creatures into that ruined look you like. I had them plated so only the copper shows. The green in the glass will become more interesting as the piece ages."

"I can't believe you made this for us." John refused to react to the announcement that the table was her final piece of welding. So the house and its yard still belonged only to her. She would install the furnace and cast her work in the backyard despite his objections.

"I made it for you, John. It's another bit of your precious Venice right here in our home." Nona's tone sharpened, her old impatience at John's Venetian obsession tarnishing her gift.

"It's amazing, sister mine, absolutely amazing. I'm so honored to be here for its debut that I'm running out to purchase an appropriate bottle of champagne. We can even purée some peaches and make Bellinis."

Al grabbed a Giants cap from the hat tree by the front door. "Hey, how did you get this thing in here, Nona?"

"Matthew drafted a couple of his art-moving buddies." Nona knotted the hem of her long black T-shirt.

John looked away from the table for the first time to question his wife, "Matthew was just here? Why didn't he say hello?"

"We didn't want to spoil the surprise, silly. You think our old chairs will work with this?"

John looked at her for a long moment before he nodded.

"I'm off to buy bubbles. Anything else?"

"Get a couple of bottles, Al." John reached for his wallet.

"Forget the money." Al shut the front door behind him.

"It's so elegant, Nona. You've made my mythological creatures stark and modern somehow. I'm enormously impressed."

John reached for Nona, feeling the tightness in her back that seemed to reproach him for being impressed rather than delighted. But the griffins were too fierce for delight, appearing more like beasts waiting to attack than peaceful guardians.

John massaged Nona's shoulders, his large hands kneading her carapace of stubborn tension.

"How much weight will the table hold, Nona? Let's welcome it into the house while your brother's out."

"We haven't made love on a new piece of furniture in years, John, never mind a piece of art. I'm filthy; all I want is a shower before dinner." She squirmed out of John's reach when he kissed her salty throat.

At the foot of the stairs, Nona glanced at her Eames chair in the living room in defiant homage to a nightmare she'd had on their honeymoon.

John had towered over her, wearing the robes of a medieval abbess, with the wings of his headdress jabbing through the ceiling and shattering the wood. Moving slowly to the strains of a Gregorian rap, her new husband had artfully arranged antimacassars and needlepoint pillows all over her most treasured piece of furniture. The music had drowned her objections as she'd watched her beloved chair disappear under luxurious layers of decoration. Years later, the dream still scratched at her like synthetic lace.

Nona stood under the shower until the bathroom was foggier than the Sunset. For the first time in days, she left her sweaty work clothes in a tired heap in the corner. She would dress up for dinner, wear the dress John always admired. The new table was an occasion.

A short black dress tugged over her head, Nona opened the curtains and looked down on John's garden. On her property. A New York native, she'd moved to California when a maiden aunt left her this house in North Beach, maiden perhaps a misleading descriptor, since the house had been given to Aunt Theresa by the restaurant owner whose mistress she'd been for twenty-six years.

Nona burrowed into the depths of her closet. She stepped into the highest pair of the heels she saved for openings and parties. She'd kept her hair short, her clothes black, and her lips red, but finally surrendered her contention that real women wore heels every day to the calf-wrenching inclines of Telegraph Hill.

Nona had watched the gradual softening of her New York edges with suspicion, too besotted by the light, the beautiful house, and the availability of cheap studio space in her new city to keep to her original plan of selling the house and returning to New York.

She reached for her makeup. Dinner would be their own private opening.

Al put two bottles of champagne in the fridge and stared at John's work. "You sure she's gonna like this, man?"

The spotlights were dimmed and candles on the table reflected in the french doors, the tabletop, and the room's many mirrors. Small flames flickered mysterious messages around the room. An antique lace runner bisected Nona's table. Red roses spilled out of a crystal vase centered on the runner.

"What? She loves these roses." John added three more flowers to his arrangement.

Nona's heels clattered down the stairs. She grabbed at her favorite chair when she saw the dining room.

"So you broke the table in without me, John?"

"You love the smell of these roses, dear wife."

"It's lovely. Where's the champagne?" Nona walked quickly into the dining room. The flowers' wanton perfume drowned the sharp smell of metal, a scent she'd wear if someone bottled it.

"Did you want to break a bottle against the table?"

"Oh, Nona. I don't. . . ." John's voice flattened into silence.

Al opened the champagne without explosion and filled three flutes.

"To art." Al raised his glass.

"To Nona." John raised his.

"To fucking and eternal Venice." Nona clanged her flute against the men's glasses hard enough to mimic a cable car's bells clamoring through the room. She drained her glass and declared she was ravenous.

John promised dinner within twenty minutes. He insisted he didn't need help. Boiling water for pasta in the kitchen, John worried the foggy steam would wander to condense on Nona's tabletop. He chopped a handful of herbs from the garden and added them to the tomatoes he'd simmered all afternoon. Bright leaves floated on the thick crimson sauce. Nona would object if he enriched the sauce with even a splash of cream. Slowly stirring, he banished images of splattered red above the griffins' beaks.

John remembered teaching Nona that early Venetian artisans used arsenic to tint their glass green.

Coyote

Peg Ellingson

The summer I began menstruating, my grandmother, Mable Stjernquist, told me one of her prairie stories. At that time, she must have been nearly seventy. My Aunt Alice, who had always lived with her, took the Pekingese dogs out for a long walk, and Grandma and I spent the last of the afternoon on her small patio in the Sierra foothills, admiring her fuchsias and their hummingbirds.

"There was this girl, Bernice," she began. Her forefinger and thumb framed her face, a familiar gesture when she was thinking. "Like me, she was holding down a claim."

Grandma had been raised in Wyoming, in the rolling hills just southeast of Cheyenne, an area called "The Golden Prairie." From the photographs I'd seen, all of them taken after her marriage, I knew that she had always been plain and somewhat forbidding, a wiry woman with a characteristic worried expression, as though she continually suffered some private misfortune. As a young woman, she moved alone to a homestead near the one her folks had already proved up on. She taught school at a rough-hewn shanty about three miles from her own shack. Most everywhere she went she rode Midge, her Indian pony, back and forth to school in good weather, down the hill several miles to see her folks, or fast through the night to the barn dances at Campstool. She was twenty-two in 1910 when Halley's Comet arced its silver path across the sky. The prairie was beautiful, lonely and wild, and Mable was as free as a woman could be back then.

Grandma didn't like to talk about personal troubles, such as my grandfather, Oscar Stjernquist. Later, in her nineties, she remembered him with affection, but during my childhood, questions about him and men in general were met with silence. About the only thing Mom and Grandma could agree on was not talking about Oscar.

One reason my mother did not get on with Grandma Mable was probably because they were too much alike, but Mom encouraged the special bond Grandma and I shared. The summer Grandma told me the story, my parents had allowed me to fly up to visit her. I felt quite grown up. Of course I didn't tell Grandma about starting my period, but somehow she sensed a change.

"I thought you were the only one who homesteaded alone," I reminded her. "You never told me about Bernice." A hummingbird hovered on the edge of my vision, an iridescent blur.

Grandma pondered my comment. "She had a brother but he'd gone back east. So she was alone for a spell. Bernice taught school too—that's how lots of the single women got by on homesteads rather than raising crops—are you going to listen or not?" Her voice edged with annoyance, and I had to beg to get her going again. I had heard happy tales of pony races and dances and terrifying stories of people caught in prairie fires or lost in blizzards. But this story was new.

It was late spring and Bernice was fixing supper, boiled potatoes probably—it was too early for greens—and possibly a little piece of salted meat. She had already filled the water trough from the nearby creek down the path behind her little shack, then drawn some for herself. While the potatoes boiled on the wood range, Bernice stepped outside. Perhaps she saw it was getting dark and wanted to close up the chickens—coyotes were always a danger at night. It was then she saw a man leading his horse to the water trough in her yard. Her own horse, grazing on her line, lifted her head and nickered.

Bernice didn't like strangers coming on her land, and she was alone. Sensing her, the stranger looked up and called a greeting. He cleared his throat, like he hadn't used his voice in a while, then told her he was just passing through, and asked if he could sleep over in the yard that night. She stood there, not knowing what to say. "My brother and I are here," she blurted. "But right now he's gone."

"I see," said the man, finally. She reset a hairpin nervously as he told her that he was headed to New York. Then she went back in the shanty and turned the meat.

The light changed and she realized he was standing in the doorway. "Smells good," he said. "Could I do chores for some of that hot food?"

He seemed friendly enough, though she didn't like his eyes. Still, it would be unchristian not to agree. He went to tend the livestock while she peeled some more potatoes and fried them along with another piece of meat. When she heard him splitting kindling, she fixed some gravy, enough for breakfast the next morning, too. She had set the table and lit the lamp by the time he came back. He dropped his gear outside except for the rifle, which he set just inside the shanty door. He had washed up, hair and beard slicked down. His rolled sleeves revealed heavy arms.

Bernice eyed the gun, and he noticed. "Just in case that coyote comes around."

He told her that he had shot a female coyote dead several days before at sundown. It was unusual to have one approach, but he must have been close to her den. He'd traveled on a ways, then stopped for the night. But he'd hardly slept, kept awake by another coyote howling. "Her mate," the man grinned. "He's been following me ever since, but never comes close enough for me to shoot him. Coyotes know when you have a gun."

They fell silent while eating dinner, as if the man had used up his quota of words telling the story. In her mind's eye she thought about her brother's rifle, which was with her brother. The man's arm shifted on the table, next to the dinner plate, her dinner, her plate, her home. Washing up, she lifted the skillet from the stove, and felt him watching. She turned back to her pan of dishwater, filled with panic.

Grandma paused in her storytelling and reached in her pocket for her handkerchief. She blew her nose and watched the hummingbirds thoughtfully.

"What happened?"

A stony look came over her face. "She should have known better, maybe, but he had caught her off guard. Of course he tried to have his way with her."

How else would the last of the Victorians describe it? I saw her struggling against him in the small cabin, the man shoving her toward the quilted bed, pressing her down. I was only thirteen, and my mind went blank.

Then Grandma went on. Bernice tore away from him and without being conscious of what she was doing, leaped to the door and grabbed the rifle before he could stand. She warned him not to move, but he apparently didn't think she would pull the trigger. She didn't think she would either, but when he lunged for her, the gun fired. His face disappeared in the bloody explosion and he dropped to the floor. It was a gruesome place to put a bullet at close range.

"What?" I couldn't believe what I was hearing. "Did he die?"

"Oh, yes, he died right away. She didn't mean to kill him, you know, but she was terrified. And she wasn't used to shooting a gun."

"You never told me this story," I said, almost accusingly. "Why haven't you told me this before?"

Grandma shot me a piercing glance. "Not a story for a little girl. But you're not so little any more, are you, missy?" Beyond the porch, a neighbor turned on sprinklers, and we were quiet for awhile. My mind whirled. "Besides," she went on, "Bernice didn't want anyone to know."

"Then how did you find out?"

"I was the only one she ever told. She couldn't keep

it to herself forever. You have to tell something like that." Grandma tilted her head. "Do you want to hear the rest of it or not?"

Poor Bernice huddled on the bed that whole night, trying not to look at the horror on the shanty floor. At first she thought of saddling her horse and riding straight to town. But then she imagined the sheriff and the questions, the talk, the shame. What if this man were someone important? Would they believe what happened? It had all happened so fast, her life ruined in an instant.

Then she remembered what he had done and the anger rushed in. By first light, Bernice had made a decision. She might never be the same, but he was not going to ruin her life further. She struggled the stiffening corpse onto a muslin sheet. Gasping with the effort, she pulled the sheet through the open door and over to the path that led down to the creek. The sun wasn't even up yet. Bernice stopped halfway down the path, out of breath. Glancing up, she saw the coyote silhouetted against the dark blue sky, watching her, the hair on its neck standing in a thick ruff, its eyes glittering in dawn shadow. It followed her to the creek and watched from a distance as she dug in the soft dirt. She was vaguely alarmed by the animal's presence, but she had more pressing concerns. Eventually, it slipped away.

She stopped after awhile to tend to the animals. Since the coyote had disappeared, she let the chickens into their wire enclosure. She fed her horse and staked the cow. The prairie looked so fresh and clean in the morning light that it didn't seem possible such a monstrous thing had occurred. She forced herself back down the path to finish the task. It took her until nearly noon to dig the hole; then she dragged the sheet to the edge and rolled the body in. When she was finished with the grave, she used his saddle on her horse, bundled his gear behind her, and, leading his horse, headed west.

Bernice rode for a long time. When she was far away, she unharnessed his horse and chased it off. At last she came to a rocky, brush-filled ravine. Dismounting, she fumbled at knots, aware of the sun slipping down the sky, then started into the chasm. She found a rock from which she could roll his gear down to the creek at the bottom where it would be scattered when the rains came. The tears started as she climbed out, and she continued to weep as she took the stranger's saddle from her horse and threw it down the slope. She leaned against her horse's neck and sobbed, then stopped abruptly as she heard a noise and looked up. Above her, on a rock, the coyote stared back at her.

All the way home, she glanced back to see him following her at a respectful distance, trotting in that odd, gangly way coyotes have. She wondered why he was acting that way, but she sensed he meant no harm.

That night in her cabin, she heard him howling, as though far away. Then suddenly he was close, passing the shanty on the path to the creek, yipping as he went, small insistent sounds, as though he were trying to tell her something. All that summer and fall he hung around, following her a mile or two if she took the horse and went to see her folks or into town. In the autumn he followed her to school and back, even after the snows. One day toward spring she noticed he was gone.

Grandma cut off the story as Aunt Alice unlatched the gate and their little Pekingese dogs filled the yard. I followed a shimmering emerald bird as it whirred away from the porch, my mind aflame with the story. Had Bernice ever confessed to the authorities about killing her tormentor? What had he done to her on that bed? If it was really awful, then she had every right to defend herself, didn't she? And why did the coyote hang around? All that night I waited for a chance for Grandma to continue, but her mood had changed, and she clearly didn't want to talk about it. I did ask Aunt Alice the next day when we were shopping together about Grandma's friend Bernice. She shrugged. "We had a neighbor in Iowa named Bernice," she offered. She didn't know about a Wyoming Bernice.

A few days later, as I took the plane back to southern California, I went over the story, wondering again about the coyote, what he wanted. Bernice must have missed him by the time he went away. And why did Grandma tell me that story? She said Bernice should have known better, but what was it she should have known?

Then I was back in Redondo Beach where I lived with my parents and older sister. The evening I returned my mother had been drinking and an argument flared up with my father. Later that night, I argued with my first boyfriend, a sweet, goofy surfer whom I accused of being disloyal while I was gone. It was improbable and unfair of me to make the accusation. After I had apologized, he asked me why I was always flying off the handle, a question I didn't know how to answer.

A few nights later when my mother was drinking again, I asked her if she had ever heard about Grandma's story of Bernice who shot and killed a man who attacked her.

"In Wyoming?" My mother shook her head. "No. But I know about a woman who shot her husband because he hit her. Shot him in the leg. A parting shot. That was the end of that marriage."

"Who's that?"

"Never you mind." She picked up her glass. "Don't ask." The look on her face persuaded me to obey. That was how she often conveyed family stories, by innuendo.

Like Grandma, my mother seemed possessed by some harsh grief. She seemed continually armed against the world, waves of anger rising apparently from nowhere, anger which she seemed unable to control. Things would appear calm, rolling along, then a tsunami of rage would swell and crash on whoever was near, my father usually, but also on my sister, Mary, and me, and mostly on Mary, because she and Mom were so much alike.

After that summer trip I didn't see much of Grandma. Sometimes we'd drive up for Thanksgiving or Christmas, but then Mom would fight with her and a year or two would go by before someone would venture a truce. Besides, by then I was moving into my life.

I dated a lot, moving from one relationship to the next as soon as things turned rocky. In college, the man I considered my first true love pointed out one night that we were either arguing or getting over an argument, and he was tired of the pattern. But the pattern persisted while I finished college, went to Europe, then moved to northern California. Then, like my sister, who had married a few years earlier, I met the man I believed was perfect for me. Naturally, Mary and I had both settled on men very much like our father—kind, dependable, and utterly impenetrable, like stones. However, we were determined to make our marriages happier than the one we had witnessed as children. We would never drink or be moody. We'd take the good part of our mother—charismatic, generous and imaginative—and enlarge on it. More than anything, we wanted to spare our own children the unpredictable, frightening moments that had characterized our home during adolescence.

After I married, my husband and I settled in Santa Rosa, several hours away from Grandma. By then, I had come to realize that my family had problems they did not wish to acknowledge, and visits with Grandma meant a day with a critical, crabby old woman. Yet, despite her volatile temperament—that strange combination of enthusiasm and bitterness, which my mother had inherited—I still considered her the beloved matriarch. In her late eighties, she took up bicycle riding—a three-wheeler—and enrolled in a class to learn the new math. "Have to keep up," she'd say. She read voraciously. She made quilts from scraps and soap from lard.

Now Bernice's tale was long forgotten and I remembered only the good stories my grandmother had told me, such as the first time she saw my grandfather, dancing all night to Halley's Comet, real candles on the Christmas trees. Once I asked her to tell some prairie stories, but she shook her head. "No," she said. "I don't want to think about the past. It's today that counts." She glanced at my swollen belly. "It's the generation to come that counts."

The babies arrived, and once again our trips to see my Grandma Mable became more frequent. She made doll clothes for my daughter and cookies for my son. For Christmas one year she gave me a rag rug she had crocheted in a huge oval. Her house was filled with sewing projects, cross-stitched tablecloths and quilts. Once, when I was telling a friend about Grandma's life, she suggested I try to tape her stories.

She refused, then grudgingly agreed. The stories came in a thin trickle until she forgot the tape recorder. Then the trickle turned into an unending stream of spring blizzards and wheat crops and riding her pony to the schoolhouse to teach nine children to read. In the spring she planted pole beans and potatoes, and in the summer she hauled water in barrels up from her folks' claim when her creek ran dry.

Now when I drove up for a visit, she met me at the door with a sheaf of notes, watching eagerly as I plugged in the recorder. Once after a blizzard she found her chickens alive because they had beat out a space around them with their wings as the snow packed in. Coyotes were so clever they'd steal a chicken from right under your nose if they had a mind to. A coyote was the smartest, most loyal, animal that ever lived. They mated for life. Turkeys were so stupid they ran squawking when a cloud passed over the sun until they were lost. I turned the tape over and Grandma moved on to Iowa. She nursed Alice through rheumatic fever, the Des Moines River flooded, she grew food and took whatever work she could find. Then suddenly she looped back to the prairie and she was talking about coyotes.

Oh, they were thick in that country. They would sing all night, set up such a howl. In the winters, she would walk to school along the ridges to keep out of the snow, which piled up in the canyons below. One winter, a coyote walked every day with her to school and back, along the next ridge, parallel to hers. He'd trail her for a mile and a half or so. She thought he just wanted some company. Once a pack of them padded past her shack to feed on a dead animal down by the creek and they were crying and yipping, just like a bunch of children.

"Wait!" I blurted, stopping the tape. "That story about Bernice, a coyote followed her, too. Remember? Along the ridge, just like the one that followed you to school."

Grandma looked annoyed. I took a breath and went on. "We haven't recorded the story about Bernice."

"Oh. Well, I don't want to," she said irritably, reaching for her cane.

"But it's an important story, Grandma. You know, about the man who attacked her and she shot him in the face, then—"

"Yes, yes, I know what I said, but now I'm not sure. Maybe she just wished she had killed him because of what he had done to her. She just never got over it, so maybe she made that up to make herself feel better." She paused. "And Bernice isn't here to say."

"But all those details, the coyotes—"

Grandma was out of her chair and hobbling to the kitchen. "Now look at that, I've been running on and it's lunchtime. You take Rosie out while I make some egg salad. Alice will be here soon."

I walked the current Pekingese, determined to get the truth out of Grandma the next session, but it turned out to be the last tape I made. She was ill off and on, querulous and distracted, and my own life was in turmoil. For a while, we exchanged short, obligatory phone conversations.

The years passed. Cataracts plagued her; Alice bought her mother books on tape. Grandma's daily walks shortened, then stopped. She had difficulty sleeping, sometimes resting only a few hours at a time. She could no longer sew her quilts and eventually her arthritic hands refused even to crochet.

Around this time, my marriage failed. I received loving support from many friends and even from my mother, widowed now and calm. But when Grandma heard the news, she telephoned. "First your sister and now you. What could he have done to make you angry enough to divorce him?" she demanded in her high, cracked voice. "What's the matter with you, anyway?"

I was hurt, then suddenly enraged. "I didn't think you wanted to hear all the details, but how dare you blame me without knowing what's going on? Besides, you're one to talk. I never knew my grandfather because of you. You're the one who told me to watch out for men." My anger swelled out of control. I didn't understand half of what I was saying. "All the women in this family have fought back one way or another, sooner or later." I lashed her with my words, all hope of reasonable explanation lost. "Why should I be any different?"

She hung up on me, and it was months before we spoke again. By then, when I called her before her hundredth birthday, she seemed to have forgotten the phone conversation.

One hot July day, Aunt Alice telephoned. "I think you'd better come. She's drifting."

Grandma was about to turn 102. I found her in the small, pleasant bedroom at the back of the house, sleeping. Through the open, screened window I could see the porch with its rows of hanging fuchsias and the golden-green flash of hummingbirds. Her hands rested on a quilt they had made, the knuckles swollen, stretching the translucent skin across the bone. Veins like blue yarn unravelled down her wrists. The fingers of her right hand ended on a square of white cotton specked with tiny cherries, from a sundress my mother had worn when I was a small child. Her feet made a mound of a piece of my old plaid jumper, and there was her own navy blue suit, there Aunt Alice's circle skirt with the wild rose pattern, her green checked robe. I stared at her hands, thinking of all they had done. With all her long life, I sensed there was so much held in, unsaid, unlived. That's what I felt I had of my grandmother, bits and pieces of her life, moments stitched together, whole years gone.

"Oh, there you are. My girl." Her eyes on my face, the thin mouth barely moving. Her hand stirred on the quilt. I reached over and covered it with mine.

"Grandma."

"What time is it?"

"Late afternoon. The hummers are out. There's a nice breeze coming through the window."

"I feel it." She sighed. We sat for a moment in silence. She may have dozed. Then, "He's such a comfort."

I looked doubtfully at the Pekingese snoring on the quilt, its feathery tail resting on a square of my mother's sundress.

"That's Rosie, Grandma."

Her milky eyes followed my glance, then the wrinkled lids slipped down. "What was I thinking? Oh. Not her."

Warm wind swept through the sheer curtains and around the little room. "Not her. Him. I've been dreaming. You know, that autumn, when school began. He followed along on the other side of the ridge. He'd drop away the bend before, then on the way home there he'd be."

"Yes. Well, he was alone. He was lonely, grieving."

"So was I." Silence. Then again, in her weak whisper, "He knew. He stayed with me, following on the other side of the ridge. Even after the snow came. He never meant any harm. Not him." Her eyes remained closed and I saw what she was seeing. A ruff of yellow fur, a thick tail behind slender legs, golden eyes in a sharp face watching.

I swallowed. "And then you married Oscar?"

She turned her head away. "Hush now. I'm tired."

After a while I leaned down and kissed her cheek, but she had dozed off. I sat there, wondering what our lives might have been if she had set to rest what had happened that day.

Later, after she died, I realized that she had been trying to explain it to herself all along, whether she wanted to or not. My mother's reservoir of rage, Aunt Alice's celibate choice, my divorce. Through all of us, for all those years, she had been telling that story. She is still telling it.

History

Suzanne Maxson

In Beirut, Annie came down to the water to swim. The beach made a narrow pebbly crescent scattered with canvas chairs, quiet except for the soft slow lapping of water across the rocks, the water perfectly transparent, lit by the stone-bright bottom sloping into sky. She could see bottom, even beyond her depth. She waded out into this light until it gathered at her waist, until, glancing back in case Dan, her dad, might be calling her, she saw she'd come farther from shore than she'd ever ventured. But she wasn't afraid. She wanted to swim, and Dan was reading. She turned toward the bright rock-bottom shining right through her own feet. She let herself fall into the light, and she floated under water on that light into the sky.

White sky—that's all she could see from the back seat of the taxi. The quiet driver rolled his window down, rolled his white shirt sleeves up and rested his hand on the roof of the white car, a Vauxhall. Her father's arm stretched across the back of the seat and she liked it there, red hairs and freckles; sometimes he turned to smile at her, exposing the gold of his bridge-work. She tried not to be carsick.

They were on the road to Bethlehem and the wind on her face was hot. "Monty," she murmured into it, not intending to speak but reminded of poor Monty the Talking Horse back home in California, retired from performing and abandoned to pasture at Grandpa's. Monty's hooves had overgrown, curled up in rough moon-scoops. His coat was the same mottled white as the sky and she missed him.

Annie Neely, nine years old. She suspected she might wake soon from being "overseas," recall it for a while in odd bits and fragments if she tried, like any dream. Or that she was making up a story, "Overseas," which, when it ended, would be hers to tell to strangers back home in a life that smelled like Grandpa's yellow Chevy, so unlike this foreign taxi.

Dan Neely worked for Standard Oil, and in 1956 he'd taken a two-year contract to the Abadan Refinery on the Persian Gulf. S.O. paid for a nanny, a cook, a silent houseboy and a bungalow in the compound called Bawarda. They paid for holidays, like this one to Beirut, with a side trip to the Holy Land.

In Beirut, at a place called Uncle Sam's, you could get a milkshake made with real milk and a burger on a bun. She'd been content there, sucking cold vanilla through a paper straw, but she'd been hauled away on long drives in rented cars: to pose for photographs at Baalbek on the matted back of a camel, to climb "the Temple of Bacchus," to view "the Cedars of Lebanon"—Dan intoned these phrases solemnly as they approached the sites. He stayed up late in their hotel room, sipping bottles of warm Dutch beer, to study the maps and guidebooks. They always hired a guide to drive them, but Dan didn't like to be ignorant. His favorite subject in school, before the Navy, was geography; he liked to sit with Annie on the davenport, the world globe between them, pointing out to her some places he'd seen and some he'd only heard about. Before they left for Abadan he'd marked their route with threads of white adhesive tape. "Halfway around the world," he'd whispered, tracing their path with her finger—to Winnipeg, across the Arctic Circle, down to the Persian Gulf and Abadan. Annie enjoyed the sound of these words, and in bed at night she lifted her arm to write them on the dark.

They'd left Beirut for two days in Jerusalem, where father and daughter rose early to view the sites. Dan had made a list of the places he wanted to see. "Very good, sir," the driver said, folding the list into his pocket. They viewed the Church of the Holy Sepulchre, and in its cool pillared passages two priests swinging censers. "They're Greek, Anno. That's myrrh. Remember the Wise Men? That's the stuff." Then through yet another passageway and farther into darkness, a place called the Prison. The light hurt her eyes when she stepped outside. And then the Church of the Redeemer and the Via Dolorosa, Mount Moriah, the Dome of the Rock, the Pool of Bethesda. Annie mouthed these place names, recombining and repeating them like jump-rope rhymes.

The Wailing Wall, another Wall, a Gate. Dan took photographs and Annie, when she was in one, adopted his solemn expression. They ate lunch in the shade of a single tree, roast beef sandwiches and warm sweet Coca-Cola. And then the Garden of Gethsemane—she repeated the words out loud, over and over, in the back of the taxi, stirred to something like anticipation because she'd seen it in the *Big Book of Bible Stories for Children* at the dentist's office back in California. But it was nothing like that pastel grove of her expectation.

This afternoon was Bethlehem, what Annie had been waiting for—she'd been Mary in the third grade Christmas pageant. Dan had explained that the stable was really a cave, so Annie tried to picture the small gray donkeys, the cows and shepherds crowding round the baby in a candlelit cave. She imagined the smell of the cave, like Monty's neglected paddock. "Not far," the driver said, but Annie was carsick. To distract herself she strained to hear what they said in the front seat, but the wind and the engine, the tires on the road muffled their words. "1948," she heard the driver say—the year she was born. " . . . The old road . . . here is no man's land . . ."

After a while Dan glanced back and understood. "Better stop there," he told the driver. They pulled over at a dome beside the road, and Dan held her head while she gave up a clotted stream of beef and bread and Coca Cola. "That was Rachel's Tomb," Dan said soothingly, patting her hand, as they drove away. She sat up on the edge of her seat and took hold of his arm, one hand around his wristwatch and the other just above the elbow, cupping her mouth on his hairy familiar freckled arm and sucking. Then she rested her temple on the wet spot. "Feel better, sweetheart?" She nodded without lifting her head.

When Dan said "There it is!" and she roused herself to see, the town before them did actually look like the pictures in the Christmas books. So Annie was disappointed once again, when they parked in Bethlehem, to be shown not a cave but a wide empty plaza, and a small door opening into another church, with pillars, like the others, and marble, and gold-embroidered velvet. Their footsteps echoed. The guide gestured toward the altar, "Grotto is below." Down two flights of small steps, to a gloomy chamber lit with silver lamps, then down a few more steps—"Here, Anno, I think this is where the manger was." Something under glass. "You can sort of imagine how it was a cave down here," Dan offered, rather wistfully. In the town they bought a creche carved in olive wood. Then into the back seat and on to the Dead Sea.

Annie heard from the front seat, "Suez" (Dan), then "King Hussein . . . " (the driver), and Dan again, "I guess, but Russia . . . " She recalled a small map from *Newsweek* or *Time*, which Dan encouraged her to read, with "Suez" in red letters. She sat up straight, though she longed to lie down. The backs of her legs and her shoulders were wet, stuck to the slick seat cover, and the thought of her face on that plastic where the bodies of strangers had sweated was enough to keep her upright for a while. But she must have dozed. The car had stopped and Dan was opening her door.

"Here we are. The river Jordan." Annie unstuck herself from the seat and stepped into the air. She reached back for the hat and tied it under her chin. One sandal had come unbuckled and she leaned to buckle it, but Dan bent quickly to do it for her. "Hurry up. We've still got the Dead Sea and Jericho."

A current of greenish dark water, some silvery shrubs—Annie was not impressed. A few yards away a rough arbor sheltered a couple of benches and a table, and five or six men in the laced-up boots and uniforms of soldiers. They wore red and white headscarves wrapped with black cord—she'd seen them before, at the airport. Oblivious of these Americans and their guide, the soldiers laughed, legs outstretched and boots crossed, holding rifles like infants or like walking-sticks. Annie took the opportunity to stare until one noticed her, slowly raised an open palm, and smiled. She looked away.

The guide stood near the riverbank, his back to Dan and Annie, white shirt sweated to his skin. Dan took her hand and they joined him.

What they saw, beyond the river, looked at first like massive scaly hides of giant crocodiles. But the scales, yes, they were tents, row beyond row, a thousand rows, tens of thousands of brown tents in the desert. Annie looked up at Dan. Dan turned to the driver.

The driver didn't speak right away. He'd been courteous and pleasant without ever smiling, not once that she remembered. Now for the first time she wondered who he was. Did she know his name? She thought Dan had said it but she couldn't remember. After a while he turned, leaning on one leg, a hand on the back of his neck, and said, "This is refugees."

Dan frowned. "Palestinians."

"Yes. Palestinians." He turned back to the tents, and so did Dan and Annie. Refugees. She knew the word, but she couldn't remember an item from *Newsweek* or *Time* to make sense of these tents laid down into the distance, so unlike the other sites of interest. She waited for Dan to explain, but instead he headed off along the riverbank. The guide went on gazing across the water for a minute, hands in his pockets. Then he turned to Annie, making a little gesture with his head.

"Like you, miss," he said very quietly. "Children too, in the camps." Her eyes had to close and she saw the tents in rows, empty tents and a scrawny dog turning to lie down in the dust. She couldn't see the children, couldn't populate that place—"the camps"—but she understood him. She smiled at him because she didn't know what else to do. Then she ran to catch up with Dan, who took her hand and squeezed it.

"Come on, baby, it's getting late and we've got the Dead Sea. The lowest spot on earth, did I tell you that? Lower even than Death Valley."

Back in the white Vauxhall, before he started the engine, the driver turned in his seat to look at Annie and then at Dan. "This is my people," he said.

"I understand," Dan answered, but then they drove in silence to the Dead Sea.

On the last day in Beirut she went down with Dan to the water, but she didn't feel much like swimming. After a while Dan rolled his *Newsweek* into a tube and said they might as well go back to the hotel.

The Excelsior lobby was empty except for the elevator attendant, who greeted them with "*Bonjour, Monsieur, Mademoiselle.*" Dan nodded and answered, "Bon jure." The attendant smiled at Annie all the way up. He wasn't much taller than she was. The whites of his eyes were as yellow as his jagged teeth, and the sweet-herb odor on his clothing recalled the dark bazaar in Abadan, the time she'd gone there to shop for fabric with Moira Kirk and Moira's mother. Annie had worn the blue dress with the big white collar, brought from California for their second year away and still too long by a couple of inches. She loved the crispness and sheen of brand-new polished cotton, and she'd kept her eyes on the bright full skirt of that dress, at her white oxfords poking out below it. Moira's mother gripped Annie's hand too hard, squeezing her knuckles. Down there on the ground, not far from her own shoes, the misshapen, naked, ashen-dusty foot of a beggar calling *baksheesh* and reaching to tug at the blue dress. Mrs. Kirk shrieked, yanking Annie and Moira away into a stall lined with bolts of fabric, fragrant of the same sweet spicy herb that filled the elevator now.

"You learn French, Annie. French is a good language to know," Dan said to her when they stepped out at their floor. He had his hand on the top of her head, steering her toward their door at the far end of the hall. "French, and German too. You get yourself an education, not like me."

"But you know a lot, Daddy."

"Not really, baby. Not like you will. You learn to speak French." He tugged her ponytail as he said it, and then he sighed. "I'm not even much good with English. Oil—that's all I know. But you'll be *educated*." He turned the key in the lock.

Sliding the knot of his tie into place, he turned from the mirror. "Okay, then. You ready, Anno?" She was, in a blue-checked dress with a jacket that matched, white shoes and socks. She'd been hoping for one last night at Uncle Sam's, but Dan insisted on the dining room of the best hotel. The night-shift elevator man was young, with white teeth and wavy hair. She wanted this one to notice her, but he ignored her and he did not smile.

Annie was glad she'd worn the jacket. The dining room was chilly and she thought again of Uncle Sam's, the sign in English and in Arabic, red tables with bottles of real Heinz ketchup. Dan put his hand on her neck and guided her behind the maitre d' to their table. The menu was as wide and tall as an atlas of the world, and lettered in gold. The waiter bowed as he presented it. She couldn't see over it, or around it, and she couldn't find a way to hold it open without knocking down the bud vase or the glasses. Under the table her feet felt for something to rest on, but there was nothing and she had to let them dangle. When Dan announced that he would have the sole doré, Annie closed her menu and said, "Me too. Exactly the same as you. And a Coke, please."

Another waiter came to take their order. This one, too, wore white trousers and a white tight-fitting cotton jacket buttoned up around his throat. He bowed to Annie and again to her father and stepped twice backward before he turned away. Annie had grown accustomed to this deference in Abadan, not only at the Naft Club and the Golestan but at home with Aziz and Nanny and the rest. Tonight, though, she didn't like to see it. She looked down at the white linen cloth, at the napkin in her lap.

"Well, Anno, what about it? Does this beat the cabins at Lake Arrowhead or what?"

"It's much fancier."

"But that's not all, you know what I mean. This is *history*, sweetie. These places, it's something you'll never forget." He paused while the waiter poured champagne from a bottle wrapped in white cloth, emptied a small green bottle of Coca-Cola into a tumbler for Annie, and receded, bowing. Dan expanded then into his subject—how he had to join the Navy to see the world but there'd be better things for Annie, "for my girl, the future's all yours, Annie-o." Then a creamy soup. Dan held his soup spoon carefully and ladled away from himself. Annie was soothed by the movement of his freckly fingers, from soup spoon to champagne glass to a quiet fist at rest on the table. "You're not eating your soup. It's good. What's the matter?"

"Nothing. I forgot."

Then the white fish, with rice, and tiny peas, served by a third waiter, older and bald, who winked at her as he bowed. She ate the peas and the rice and broke the fish into small pieces. Dan had grown silent, distracted. He forked up his meal and chewed steadily, gesturing once for the waiter to fill his glass. Annie's own hand was trembling. She nearly spilled her Coke, saw the brown stain spreading on the white cloth before she realized that the glass was safely back on the table and nothing had happened. She folded her hands in her lap until a waiter came to take the plates.

"Okay, Annie-o, what's for dessert?" She studied the list; his attention was back with her, so she was careful to choose in a way that would make him happy.

"Hmm, it's hard to decide on the right one. I think—Peaches Melba. I've never had that."

The right answer. "Perfect! You'll love it!" This time she closed her eyes and lowered her head until the waiter was gone.

"Peaches Melba. You know, I'm not sure. Maybe I

was thinking of something else. Cobbler, I guess. With the crust? But they know what they're doing. It'll be good."

It had something to do with the waiters, she decided. Or their clothes, the white clothes and the white cloth on the table, the white tables. What are they bowing for? Why should they have to bow? She waited for Dan to answer but he kept on talking, he didn't appear to have heard her, and she realized that she had not actually spoken. Then Dan's eyes opened wide and he made a little mouth like "ooh" as the waiter appeared with Peaches Melba, placing it on the table before her, just so. She shut her eyes tight but when she opened them it was still there—the terrible glistening peach on white cream, the sauce a deep red stain.

"Anno? Annie, what?" She lifted her spoon. "What's *wrong*?"

She swallowed it.

woman in a faded kimono
MJ '95

The Window

One who lived alone, a woman
in a faded blue kimono,
at a table in a kitchen
where the spilt sugar sparkled
on a poppy-red cloth.

Reached into light
for a jade-green plate,
and a flash of hot copper
through the apricot jam
lit the hairs of her arm, and her hand
fell open,
                    filled

with light. It answered
her desire.
Love may require
the willingness of light.

– *Suzanne Maxson*

All Come Free

Susan
Pringle Cohan

Prologue

"You have reached the Pringle house. No one is in to take your call. Please leave your name and the last time to reach you. Now, wait a minute. Please leave your number at the beat."

"Hello, I'm at the country club in Las Vegas. Would someone come by and pick me up? I'd like to come home now."

"I'm here at the train depot in Salinas. Please come pick me up. I can't find my car."

"Someone, please answer. I'm in Bakersfield at a gas station, and I need you to come get me."

"Where is everybody? Please come get me. I need to get home and feed the dogs."

"Won't somebody come find me? I'm lost here in the desert.

Please someone answer."

"I'm all alone here in this strange land and I want to go home. Come save me. I don't know where I am."

"They've taken me prisoner here in Siberia. I'm afraid they're not going to feed us. Please come free me. I'm so tired and hungry."

"Oh, someone. Please, take me out of here."

"Help. Take me home. *I want to go home."*

Betsy's children listened to forty-three similar messages from their mother during her first week in the convalescent hospital.

Room 309

Clutching her sheer pink nightgown to her bosom, she peers around the corner of the industrial kitchen, her bare feet straddled wide for balance, her cane forgotten in her bedroom. She noticed the new cook at dinner tonight and knew he was trying to do his best, offering a special dessert of cherry mousse for the silent group. No one spoke at meals, although a piano player sometimes played while they ate. Some needed the nurses to feed them. She certainly didn't need help. She found most of the residents quite cross and disagreeable.

She had dutifully retired to her room after supper. Once inside Room 309, she allowed the night nurse to help her undress for bed. Her daughter called just as she was falling asleep. Susie was coming down this weekend.

"Oh, yes! In two days!" She must write it down on her calendar. But where was her calendar? And where was she at this moment? Would her daughter know where to find her? She must make a plan. She got up and surveyed the room.

This is so strange. I don't recognize this room. This isn't my furniture. And where is Susie? She just called. Is she coming now? I just talked to her. Where is my calendar? Oh, won't somebody help me? Must find someone. Where?

She gropes down the dimly lit hallway, under crystal chandeliers and prints of Monet and Degas, down the floral path of garlands in the carpet. Must find someone to help me, get me out of here. HOME!

Through the darkened dining room to the kitchen. Yes, oh, some ice cream would be good right now. To taste some smooth, rich, creamy, frozen softness. Comfort.

Peering around the corner, she sees the cook outside, dumping the garbage.

Now, wait a minute. Quick!

With renewed strength, she yanks open the heavy freezer door and grabs the gallon of chocolate ice cream. Steadying herself briefly against the steely front of the refrigerator, she hurries out of the kitchen, clutching the frozen treasure to her chest.

Now. Where is home? Through the dining room, down here, down this hall?

The cook catches a glance of lace and satin through the back kitchen window and sees her heading through the dining room toward the long hall.

"Es Señora Pringle? O, Dios! Que pasa?"

Eager to please, he grabs a large serving spoon from the tray by the sink and silently follows, as she sneaks slowly to her room. She hesitates at each door, shakes her head quizzically, and then moves on, looking for home. At last, at Room 309, she recognizes her own watercolor on the wall and scuttles to her bed, the gallon clutched in both hands. She shifts onto her bed and gleefully opens the container.

But, oh! No spoon!

Timidly, the cook opens the door. She sits, illuminated by the light of a single lamp, the gallon of ice cream on her lap. Carefully, slowly, he knocks, and enters.

"A spoon, Señora, for your ice cream?"

All Come Free

They were sitting on the only furniture still in the house, two stools at the kitchen counter. Their voices echoed against the freshly enameled white walls. Paint-spattered drop cloths covered the kitchen floor, a lone light bulb glared an unnatural light from the ceiling. Susan was examining the daily work log. Bill was pouring wine into mason jars. Her brother looked a bit crusty around the edges tonight, a three-day stubble bristling on his face, his long and thinning blond hair yanked back with a hair tie. His glass eye floated and his good eye was slightly glazed.

They had removed every piece of furniture in their mother's 4,000-square-foot Montecito house in one week. Their sister, Penny, had come from the East Coast to help with the initial stages. The art expert, she was responsible for labeling all the fine arts destined for storage.

They had had trouble figuring out what to do with

the nude male sculptures Mother had placed strategically throughout her garden. They were proud products of a growing passion for sculpturing which had recently replaced a thirty-five-year career of oil and watercolor painting.

The three of them had worked into the night. They sifted through every aspect of their mother's life, piece by piece, memory by memory. For the first time since childhood, they were alone together. No spouses, none of their own children, and no mother to act as the continual hostess. They laughed and cried over memories buried deep under layers of adulthood and their own parenting.

After Penny had left, Bill and Susan sat in the kitchen in semi-shock.

"She's not even dead yet, but it feels like we're those crones in *Zorba the Greek,*" said Susan. "It's creepy."

"I know," Billy said, "but it has to be done. We have to rent out this house. Soon."

Susan knew he was right but it was so hard to see all this beauty, twenty-seven years of an entire life, gone in a matter of days.

She sipped her wine. As newly appointed trustee of the estate, she planned to stay here for at least two more weeks. Her family and job in northern California could wait. Billy would do most of the carpentry and oversee the subcontractors. Susan would pay the bills.

"I still feel incredibly guilty for doing this." Susan swirled her wine. "It feels like we've put Mother in prison and taken the key."

"I know," said her brother, "but you've got to lighten up on yourself. Mother can't live here anymore. We know it, the doctors know it, and, deep inside, she knows it."

"Billy, I almost forgot to tell you. You remember Tini Early, Mother's lifelong friend from Carmel? She called yesterday, wanting to know about Mother. I told her what had happened, and then there was this pause on the phone. I asked what was wrong."

"Tini said, 'I promised Betsy I'd never tell you this, but she confessed to me that when she drove up here last summer, she had suddenly gotten very tired, right there on Hot Springs in Montecito, and decided to pull over for a little nap. The next thing she remembered was pulling into her cottage in Carmel.' That's 300 miles, in total blackout."

Susan exhales, "So, she's known and been hiding it for that long."

"I believe it, Sis. Remember how she managed to crash both cars a few months ago in the space of ten minutes, right here on her own property? We wouldn't have known if the gardener hadn't witnessed it. It's been a chain of events, spiraling down."

"But, Billy, it kills me she never talked about it to us. When I was down last month to help with her overdrawn accounts, she was completely defensive. The final straw was when she picked up a coin from the kitchen floor and shoved it at me, saying, 'Here, Susie, a dime for all your efforts.' I was beside myself. I almost strangled her. Later, when I'd settled down, I gave her a hug and told her, 'Denial is not a river in Egypt, my mother.' She looked at me and there was this moment of truth between us. We both laughed, almost hysterically."

"She does have these windows, doesn't she, when she could give a dinner party for twelve, no problem. But, they don't last more than five to ten minutes, Sis, before she's gone again. We're doing the right thing. Trust me."

"The hardest thing now," Susan continued, "is that her things are always packed when I come to visit. It makes me feel so awful to tell her she can't leave, that she needs to unpack. When will she settle in?"

"I don't think she necessarily wants to come home. You know how she's traveled the world all her life? She wants to be prepared to go anywhere anyone wants to take her. That's why she's always packed. Remember how she always asked, 'What's the itinerary, what's the plan?' Now, she's not so sure *what* the plan is, but she knows there must be one somewhere."

Could it be her brother was right? All her life, her mother had planned every moment meticulously. Out of sheer will, she had invented her life from beginning to end. She had presented herself proudly, with dignity. How things appeared outweighed what really was. Reality had nothing to do with it.

So now, nearing the end, the only way she could keep that dignity was to be ready, ready for any journey that awaited her. Leaning over the table, Susan began to weep, sobs of compassion, for a mother whose deep pride had kept her real self from them for so long.

The Sea Cove

Betsy has all her possessions packed in a plastic laundry basket by the door when her daughter arrives. Books, nightgowns, panties, dresses, shoes are all neatly stacked in layers. Her suitcase has been removed by the nurses. The laundry basket is the only movable receptacle in her room.

Her purse and cane ready in hand, she smiles as her daughter enters the dimly lit room.

"Oh, Susie! How wonderful you're here! Where did you come from? I just got back from an ocean cruise, and, oh, what a wonderful picnic I had with my doctor! Now, what's his name, again? I know his name. Let's see. . . ."

With a resigned, whimsical look toward heaven and the gold-speckled ceiling, she shrugs. "You know, I'm losing my memory a bit. I just can't seem to remember things lately. Tell me, where am I?"

"You're in Room 309, at the Cliffview Terrace, a nice hotel-hospital where you live now."

"I am? Well, *this* is news. How *long* have I been here?"

"Oh, about a month, Mother." Susan doesn't have the heart to tell her it has been almost a year.

"No! I haven't been here a month! I just arrived. And why am I here? I want to go home."

"Mother, you've had some heart attacks recently," Susan lies, "and the doctors feel you should be in a place where you can be completely cared for. And you're a little confused sometimes. At home, you'd wake up in the night and wander onto the street trying to figure out where you were."

"No. I *never* did that! Tell me, just where *is* my house?"

"It's here in Santa Barbara, Mother. On Hot Springs Road."

"Hot Springs Road. But I thought I lived over the mountains. You know, over the hills, where we all grew up."

"No, Mother. We haven't lived there for forty years."

"Oh, well, yes, you're right, but then, where *is* my house?"

"Here, in Santa Barbara."

"Oh, I don't know, I can't remember. What does it look like?"

Susie knows the memory clues by now. "Remember, it's the house with the big coromandel screen in the living room. And your sculptures outside overlooking the pool."

"It is? Oh, yes. The coromandel screen. Let's go now. I want to go look at my house."

"No, Mother, not today."

"But, why? I'm going home today. Didn't you come to take me out of this place? I'm all packed, as you can see." She looks proudly at her packed laundry basket and bends down to make sure it is all there. "When do we leave?"

"Not today, Mother. The doctors say you should stay here for just a little while longer."

"But, you mean, I have to stay *here*? In *this* place?"

"Yes, just for now."

"But who's paying for all of this?"

"I am, Mother."

"Oh, good! I'm so glad you're here. I don't have to worry anymore, do I?"

"No, you don't need to worry. Everything's taken care of."

"Susie, dear, I didn't know you were so responsible. I always remember you as the youngest, a tagalong to your brother and sister. When did you grow up to be such an accomplished young woman?"

"Mother, I'm forty-five. I have a husband and almost-grown children."

"You have children? Who are they? Where do you live?"

"We live in northern California, Mother. You've been there."

"I have? Can we go there now? I need to see it. Let's go there now. My bags are all packed. Tell me the plan. What's our itinerary? Let's get out of here. Take me out of here. Take me home."

"No, not today, my mother. Today, let's go to the Sea Cove, that nice place on the water where you like the clam chowder and we watch all the people on the beach."

"Oh, have we been there before? I don't think so."

"Yes, Mother. We've been there many times. All the waiters know us."

"They do? Well, yes, that sounds good. You know, I think I'll have the clam chowder."

They are seated under the heat lamps at the Sea Cove, overlooking the broadest expanse of beach and sea on the California coast. It is sunset and children play in the sand, buckets gripped in gritty hands. Lovers flirt and pause to kiss; runners heave their deep-footed way along the water's edge. Sailboats skim over the water, shimmering iridescent butterflies. It is the perfect, quintessential sunset.

"I want the clam chowder. In a bowl. No rolls," Susan's mother orders, without once looking at the young waiter.

"I'll have the Caesar," Susan says, "and a glass of white. . . ."

Betsy interrupts her daughter, "Waiter, wait a

minute. You didn't get my order. I'll have the clam chowder, in a bowl."

"Yes, ma'am. I got that. Would you like anything to drink?"

"Oh, yes. Wait a minute. A glass of tea, yes, a glass of iced tea. But I didn't order yet. I would like a bowl of clam chowder. A bowl, not a cup."

Susan shoots the waiter a look: *Please* understand. And *quick*!

Her mother is shrouded in a white wooly sweater. She looks wistfully at others already enjoying their dinners.

"Mother, look at that little child with the bucket, the one in green shorts. Isn't he cute? He reminds me of Billy when he was young."

"Oh, yes. Let me get my glasses. Oh, no. Where is my purse? Someone's taken my purse." She fumbles under her chair, a frantic look of anxiety clouding her face.

"It's right here on the table, Mother. Can I get your glasses for you?" Susan hands them to her.

"Which little boy? The one with the toy sword? But look. He's wandering off from the others. He might get lost." Susan looks across the sand to see if anyone is watching the boy. As Susan peers through the glare, her mother suddenly runs with unexpected agility towards the beach.

"Wait, Mother. It's okay. See? His older brother and sister are coming. Stop, it's all right."

Her mother freezes, first looking at the scene on the beach, then back to her daughter. "Billy, are you all right?" she says under her breath.

Susan reaches her mother's side. "It's all right, Mother. The little boy is fine. You thought for a second it really was Billy, didn't you? Did you think of the accident?"

"Yes, oh dear. I need to sit down."

"It's all right now, Mother. Billy's a grown man now. He has better vision with one eye than I do with two. It wasn't your fault."

"For years I thought it was. It was only for the second we weren't looking when it happened, you know."

"Yes, I know."

"I never forgave myself. That's partially why we had you, to help us get over the tragedy."

"I know, Mother. You've told me that too."

She rests her head down on the table. "I'm so tired."

Betsy suddenly looks up. "Oh, Susie, I'm so frightened. Of all of this. I've depended on my mind all my life. It was a good mind. And now, it's all going. I can't depend on it to remember anything. And I get so confused. I think things that happened long ago are happening now, and vice versa. The worst thing is that this could go on for years. It's not going to get better, is it? Tell me the truth."

"Mother, let's go sit over there on the beach and watch the sunset. Forget dinner. It's more important to talk."

"Yes, dinner can wait. Let's talk."

Susan leads her slowly to the beach and finds them a spot. She spreads her jacket and helps her mother sit on it. Kneeling, she embraces her mother.

"Mother, I want to soothe you as you soothed me so often when I was young, 'Don't be frightened, it's all right.' But we both know it's not all right. It's scary in there, isn't it?" She rocks her gently. Her mother starts to weep.

"Susie dear, you are so loving and kind. I always thought of you as selfish, as a sort of spoiled little girl. Which you were, you know. But that was my fault." She chuckles softly. "Now I depend on you so much. Where did you learn to take care of me like this?"

"I learned from you, my mother."

"You know, I really would like to die. I'd like to be done now. Don't be shocked. I'm not at all frightened of death. I welcome it. I believe so strongly that all my loved ones will be there to greet me. But I don't know how to die, to let go of this old body. Living in it without my mind is more frightening than dying is."

"Mother, you have a terrifically strong life force. Everyone who knows you says so. You can be dead asleep and wake up bright-eyed like a little girl, instantly ready to go, ready to do whatever's next. Do you think praying will help?"

"I pray, believe me. But I keep coming back."

"Well, I guess if you're still here, God needs you for something."

"But what could I possibly offer?"

"The nurses say you help them with some of the others who are worse off than you. You know, you're quite a bit younger than some of the others, and they have more trouble walking and moving around than you do."

"Well, if I can still help. I suppose when it's time for me to go, I'll know. But will you be here in the meantime? I feel so alone and some of those old people are so cross."

"I'll be here, my mother. I'm here."

"Oh, I love you so, darling."

And they sit, cuddled arm in arm, as the sun sets, and the lights from the derricks offshore come on and sprinkle the darkness with diamonds of light.

Sailing on a Train to the Airport

The red brocade salon steams with frail, wet heads, the smell of permanent solution fumes and the hypnotic hum of ten blow-dryers. Tuesday is beauty day at the Cliffview and the small room is packed. Betsy emerges transformed, her coiffure a perfumed puff-cloud. She feels absolutely pampered, but also resents loudly the outrageous cost for such a service.

"Imagine charging ten dollars for this hairdo! Highway robbery. Even if Susie does pay for it. Must mention it to the management."

Nevertheless, feeling very elegant and outgoing, Betsy walks down the hallway toward the dining room. "Well, good morning." Betsy beams as she rounds the corner and approaches a tiny, bird-like grey-haired woman maneuvering her way down the hall with her walker.

"How are you enjoying our lovely train trip?"

"Oh, it's marvelous, isn't it? The service is so good. The food could be better but the views are superb. I get up specially for them, you know."

"When do you think we'll arrive?"

"Well, I think at dinnertime, don't you? They'll tell us then."

"Well, I don't know. I think I'll ask this nice woman." Betsy sees the nurse heading toward them.

"Excuse me, what's your name? We want to know when we arrive."

"Oh, Mrs. Pringle and Mrs. Catherwood, good morning! Don't you both look lovely with your new hairdos! How are you both today?"

"Oh, we're fine," says Betsy, "but we want to know when we arrive."

"Arrive, Mrs. Pringle?"

"Why, yes, we're coming into the harbor soon. My friend and I want to know when the ship plans to dock."

The day nurse knows what she is doing. "Oh, in a few hours, ladies. I hope you're enjoying the trip. Would you both like a little something? Let me fix you some tea. Let's go to the dining saloon, and you can sit and visit."

"Oh, how sweet of you, dear," says Elsa. "Tea, oh yes, with cream and no sugar. Sugar is fattening, you know, and I'm watching my diet."

"Oh, yes, I know, Mrs. Catherwood. You mind your figure, don't you?" The nurse winks at her and heads for the kitchen.

"You ladies just have a seat and I'll be right back with your tea."

Betsy and Elsa sit at one of the dining tables with their porcelain cups of tea. They are surrounded by romantic Monets, Victorian women in broad garden hats and white gloves, portraits of a bygone era of propriety and order that mirrors the women who sit before them.

"My name is Elizabeth Pillsbury Pringle. But do call me Betsy. I haven't been here for long. I have a house on, wait a minute, well, in Santa Barbara. I'm going home as soon as this train trip is done."

"Pleased to make your acquaintance, Betsy. My name is Elsa Catherwood. My husband's going to meet me. He's the head of the Santa Barbara Museum. He called me last night and said he was going to meet me at the airport."

"How curious! Your husband is the head of the museum? I was a docent for fifteen years and had a small one-woman show there years ago. But I don't live there anymore. Now that I've moved north."

"Well, then, we must have met each other before. At your opening? I threw all the cocktail parties for the museum."

Betsy eyes the tiny woman, embarrassed. Had she ever met her before? She decides to fake it.

"Why, yes! Of *course,* I remember you. You were such a nice hostess. You threw the most lavish cocktail parties."

"Well, yes, I suppose I did," Elsa beams. "Those were the days, weren't they?"

"Yes, they certainly were. Such talented artists then. Not like today's art. It's all trash."

"No respect for the Masters, that's what I think," Elsa shakes her head sadly.

The conversation stops as Elsa recalls her cocktail parties and Betsy tries to remember if she has ever met the woman sitting across from her.

Waking from her reverie, Elsa asks, "Are you sure we're arriving soon? I'm afraid we've all been taken prisoners."

"Prisoners? What do you mean?"

"Well," Elsa says, "they took my watch this morning.

I can't find it anywhere."

"They took your watch? Are you sure?"

"It's not in my cabin. I've looked and looked. I've talked to the people," she eyes the kitchen, "but they just shrug. I don't think they speak English." Elsa's blue eyes cloud. She makes a smacking sound with her mouth and starts to wring her hands.

"Now, don't worry, Elsa," Betsy attempts. "Let's see. Maybe someone stole it."

"But it could be anyone on this train. We'd have to look in all the cabins."

"Well, should we look in mine? It might be in my room. Who knows?"

"Yes, it's a plan. After tea let's go look."

The Gift

The irony of it. My mother, a woman who based her entire life on control, has now lost all of it, mind and body. Once proud and unapproachable, she has returned to her childhood. In letting go, she has found love.

"I've forgotten my purse so I'm afraid I don't have anything to give you today but a kiss," she flirts with the male nurse. She gives him a peck on the lips.

He pretends to blush. "Oh, Mrs. Pringle!"

"Oh, just call me Betsy!" she grins coyly.

For me, it has been two years of continuous crises. Rent the house, pay the bills, deal with the doctors, oversee the convalescent home, hire the extra caregivers, cope with winter floods, repair the house damage, replace the tenants, pay unexpected bills.

This spring, a series of small heart attacks, pneumonia, panicked calls to ER. Should we keep her on life support? What about the living will? Where is the friggin' doctor? On the golf course?

Change doctors, watch miraculous recoveries, retrain the caregivers, hire a new daily companion.

But most of all, hold my mom. Hold on for dear life.

It's better now than a year ago when she kept trying to escape. With alarms at all the main exits, she left her patio room and found a back fence to the parking lot. She almost made it one day. She'd piled her clothes and books into her laundry basket, heaved it over the back fence, and was just climbing onto the parking lot when one of the nurses arrived. After that, they kept her restricted. No more patio bedroom. She was furious.

Then, weakened after pneumonia and several heart attacks, she is restricted to a wheelchair. Now it is too late to escape. She knows this, but still shows her token rebellion by climbing into bed with her wheelchair strapped to her back. It is her last defiance.

Home now is a concept in her mind. Going home to her is a journey in time, not space, to the home of our childhood in northern California. She is completely in the present, the past a tangled thicket of dreams and the future incomprehensible. "Let's think about all that after lunch," she says.

I am back for my third visit of the day and it's as if I've never been there. As I approach her in the dining room, she looks up and exclaims, "Oh, Susie, you're *here!* Where did you come from? How did you find me and how did you find this place?"

"Yes," I say, for the third time today. "I'm *here.*"

She looks at me intently, "But *I'm* not. Am I?"

"You look pretty here to me!"

She chuckles, then shrugs, "Oh, I'm so confused."

"It's okay. Mother. We're all here to take care of you. You go on being as confused as you want to." She looks at me. Her eyes begin to glaze.

"It's all right, Mother. Really."

In her room, I help her into bed. I bring her ice cream with fudge sauce. She eats it, ice cream smearing her cheeks, dripping sweet brown liquid onto her blouse. After she is done, I lie down beside her and snuggle up close.

"Mother, I want to tell you about a dream I had about you and I last night."

"No, you and *me,* dear," she corrects, gently. I nod, thinking she doesn't have a clue about where she is but she can still correct my grammar.

"We were dancing, Mother. Around and around. I think it was a polka. We were weeping with laughter. You were so happy. Dressed in crinoline. Then we both fell down exhausted on your bed."

"What a sweet dream, dear. Let's do it again soon."

She's looking at the weekly schedule of events across the room. It's a purple page, 11 x 17, tacked to the middle of the bulletin board on her wall.

She looks at me and says, "Susie, we must take that painting with us when we go home today. Is it a Rothko? It's so exquisite. We musn't forget."

I look carefully. The corners are curled forward from the outside edges, making shadows as if it were three-dimensional, yes, a Rothko, with mystery. As I see it through her eyes, it is strikingly beautiful.

I say, "Yes, we will be sure to take that with us when we leave."

"When do we go?" she asks for the millionth time.

"When the doctors say," I tell her for the millionth time.

"Oh, all right," she sighs. "I think I'll take a little nap now. Do you want to take a nap too?"

"Sure, Mother. Close your eyes and I'll sing you a lullaby."

chocolate chips
Something to Eat
pie
ice cream
Give me
Something to
cake

Mouth

Bonnie Olsen McDonell

He was talking about being a fat man. He'd told the same story last week, about having to buy two airline seats. His trip to New York, the famous people he knew there. He rambled on enthusiastically, trying to make eye contact with everyone, especially Noreen.

Bridget looked at her watch. She should have brought a magazine. Verbal masturbation. That's what this was. All the women politely listening while the man complains and then begins his braggadocio trip. Get a shrink. Make a continuous tape and play it back to yourself, Bud. On a walkman. For this she drove forty miles and paid money?

The lady to Bridget's left was staring at the paisley carpet. She was wearing a dress shaped like an army tent, same color too. It set off her warm maple eyes. Those warm maple eyes were staring now at the snack tray. Willing it closer, Bridget presumed. Eating from being bored stiff. She'd been there. For extended periods.

The talker droned on. How he'd tried Weight Watchers, Jenny Craig, HMR. He forgot to mention NutriSystem this week.

Couldn't someone else speak? One of these big bright women must have something to say. At home she'd have thrown open the fridge, grazed through the shelves for something tough to gnash her teeth on. Peanut brittle. But according to the syllabus, this class was going to teach them to do something new when the hunger triggers fired.

She let her eyes close, her chin rest on her chest. She slowed her breathing until it was deep and regular. Then she let out the snore, which rose from a quiet sizzle to a blasting snort. Pete had told her how to do that. Pete, who had enjoyed her letters and phone calls, but came down with the flu when he'd met her. Pete the joker. He taught kindergarten. Perhaps he preferred little girls. She snored again, a longshoreman's roar of a snore. Someone tittered, chortled. She shook herself as if to wake.

"Oh, sorry." She smiled at the group and rubbed her eyes.

Noreen, the statuesque facilitator for "Don't Weight," stood up. "Time for a break. Come on over and try some of these fat-free snacks. Remember to eat slowly."

The group edged toward the snacks. Some circled, then began to nibble the muffins and cookies; others grabbed and hustled back to their seats.

Bridget picked up a grainy muffin with blueberry stains seeping through the surface. She headed for the vanilla-scented coffee, Mr. Mouth in front of her. He fondled a cup while talking to Noreen. Bridget gripped her muffin and waited. They were supposed to eat sitting down.

Finally Mouth turned to her, "Didn't you get

enough sleep last night? It's Bridget, isn't it?"

Bridget nodded at him. "Yes on both counts." She put her cup under the silver spigot. "I sure look forward to getting to the triggered-eating cycle in part four." She looked over her shoulder at Noreen, admiring her silk tunic and double ropes of pearls.

"We may not have an opportunity to get to that tonight." Poppyseeds freckled Noreen's apologetic smile.

"That's too bad," Mouth lamented. "I had some things to say about that cycle." He stepped closer to Noreen. "Now, I've had some experience. . . ."

Bridget looked at the muffin. She really wasn't hungry. This thing was the color of baby shit and felt dense as rock. She put it back on the tray. Noreen was nodding at Mouth. The class had thirty minutes to go.

Bridget felt her shoulders tense as she headed back to her seat. A dozen pairs of eyes stared at Noreen and Mouth. The snacks were gone.

Bridget sat down, took a sip of perfumed coffee and closed her eyes trying to relax. A tremendous snore ripped forth from her. Coffee sloshed onto her black rayon skirt. She hadn't planned that one.

Maple Eyes was dabbing at Bridget's skirt with a napkin.

"Are you all right? Is this narcolepsy?" she whispered. "Do you need more air?"

Bridget felt her face flush. "No. I'm fine. Thanks." She hoped the snores were over.

Noreen and Mouth returned to the group. Noreen folded her hands in her lap. "How was that snack? Did you concentrate on tasting the food, the texture? Did you eat slowly?"

A woman with dark red hair and round green glasses cleared her throat. "I did slow down enough to taste it. I didn't like it but at least I noticed eating it."

"For me," Mouth began, "I tend to savor the kind of snacks that—"

Bridget's eyes were open when the snore exploded from her. She covered her mouth. A blush began at her toes and crept up her neck. She couldn't control them now. Perhaps if she just became very calm . . . .

"Is there something you wish to share with the group, Bridget? How was the snack for you?" Noreen smiled but her hands clenched each other into the color of nonfat milk.

"I didn't feel hungry. I didn't eat." What a concept.

Green Glasses cleared her throat. "Are you going to snore now instead of eating? Boy, I'd like my triggers to tap into something non-caloric." She offered a small smile.

Mouth opened up, "But snoring is rude. Maybe you could trade eating for smiling or deep breathing. I heard a lecture by—"

The snore was long and low, like the growl of a boxer.

Maple Eyes tucked a handful of thick dark hair behind her ears. "Keep the snore, Bridget. I'd like to borrow you sometime for our unit meetings." She laughed softly.

A gray-haired woman leaned forward. "Yeah, and when my husband starts windbagging those stories I've heard fifty times." She slapped her knee. "Dang, I'd like to let off a snore instead of rippin' open another bag of chips. My ticker'd be tickin' a lot better without a thousand miles of Fritos on its odometer."

Green Glasses rubbed her chin, leaning toward the older woman. "Can you imagine how different our lives would be if when we got angry we snored instead of ate?"

The woman next to her jangled a dark wrist full of bracelets and tapped the carpet with her bright red boot. "I'd rather sound like a bull than look like one. You are on to something, woman. All day I take crap from people; then I go home and eat crap." She shook her head. "Maybe it's time to make a little noise."

Noreen jumped up. "Well, our time is up and we certainly did leave things on a provocative note. I look forward to seeing you all next week."

Mouth rubbed his hands together. "There's something I'd like to say—"

A chorus of snores drowned him out.

Last Guard at the Gates

Franci Gallegos

She had dreamed the black boy came to kill her again. This time they were seated in an old-fashioned parlor, speaking amicably, smiling at each other. The scene was as if on a stage, their profiles in view. In back of her chair a pretty mullion-paned window, fringed with white lace curtains, revealed a tree-lined residential street and a turn-of-the-century house, its white veranda and lilac shrubs climbing up the columns and onto the sloping roof. The boy suddenly jerked his head toward the window and jumped out of his chair. He grabbed her by the back of her hair, pulling her head back so that his face was right on top of hers and she could feel his hot, angry breath mingling with her rapid gasps. He had an enormous hunting knife in his other hand. "You bitch, you set me up! You told them I would be here! I'm gonna kill you!" He put the knife at the edge of her temple the way one skins a fish. She could see his face from the corner of her eye, his tense nostrils flared, fury and hate distorting his soft, plump mouth. But his long-lashed eyes remained calm and warm, brown moons filled with love and tenderness. The knife edged under the skin at her temple and skillfully he peeled away her scalp. She tasted the salty blood flowing down her cheek and into her screaming mouth.

Lamont, don't! Lamont, please, I am your friend.

Darby jolted from her fetal curl and lay on her back like a trellised vine. She felt first the pain in her shoulders and sensed the cold and damp in the dark room. She could see the dawn as a grey backlight through the drapes, and in the spaces where the fabric did not meet she could see condensation drops on the dirt-streaked windows. Her nose, bare to the night air and feeling like cold metal, received the stale smell of must accumulated on the infrequently dusted dresser and nightstand. With pleasure, she turned her attention to her feet, warm in their comfortable nest. In the past decade of celibacy and sole occupancy of her bed she had learned to measure comfort through her feet.

She touched her temple, half expecting to feel the warm, sticky coagulation of blood. But it was dry and she relaxed her tensed body. These dreams about the beautiful Lamont had occurred almost every night for the past few weeks. Lamont—tall for his fourteen years, a luscious chocolate brown, his body filled out like a man's but his face still that of an angelic child—had entered her freshman class in midsemester. He had some trouble behind him, an assault that had sent him to juvenile hall and then a group home. He had shown her court papers one day when he was trying to explain an unexcused absence; they contained the conditions of his parole. He had to do well in school, avoid former associations, and stay away from the victim. But for all his checkered past, he was the most intelligent and original student in that racially divided, difficult fifth period.

At the very beginning of the school year, the racial tension exploded when Tajima, a devout practioner of the Nation of Islam, protested the study of *The Merchant of Venice.* Tajima appropriated the idea of ghetto as a purely black experience and demanded to know "Why we gotta read about what happen five hundred years ago? We black people live it out now." Myrna, a Jewish girl, tried to justify the play by talking about the Holocaust, but Tajima spit out her words with a barely controlled rage, "You Jews just want all the pity. Jews be livin' in the hills and we be livin' in the flatland. You Jews are rich yet whinin' about the past. But all the hurt and pain nowdays is buried in the blackman's heart." The black kids applauded. The white kids shut up. The next week Tajima transferred out of the class because it was too racist. A week later Myrna's parents placed her in a private school in the hills.

Darby could never find a way to build a bridge between the kids. Then Lamont entered the class. He had an acute intelligence and had been radicalized somewhere, perhaps through his juvenile hall experience, or maybe it was intuitive. He was steeped in revolutionary black philosophy, read *The Autobiography of Malcolm X* on his own time, and always contributed incisive commentary on the class readings. Lamont called things by their true names. "You act like a fool 'cause you're ashamed to show that you're uneducated," he told Joey, the class scoundrel. Joey tried to recover his dignity by accusing Lamont of "kissin' the white teacher's ass." "No," responded Malcolm's heir, "I intend to use my black intelligence so that the white man will be kissing my ass." The white kids paid close attention to him. He served as a role model for the less-skilled, more discouraged blacks in the class. He wrote well, did his homework, and was determined to learn. Darby loved his sense of humor, his ability to comprehend the depths of what they were reading, and his worldly understanding of the other students. Then why in God's name was he haunting her dreams, cast as her ineluctable assassin?

The insistent bell of the alarm clock shrilled, assuring her that she had survived the night and that this clouded workday morning in April was real and necessary.

First to the bathroom, although the morning pee was gratuitous after rising twice during the night to flush her dilapidated bladder. Brush her teeth, wash the sands of sleep off her face, and furtively glance at her wrecked reflection in the mirror. Oh my God, when had she first stopped noticing the split ends in her grey shag of hair? Had the liver spot under her left eye grown darker? Was there more droop to her chin? She did not dawdle before mirrors anymore since evidence of her decay was overwhelming. Aging was a process of self-renunciation, the final act of contrition.

Morning ablutions, the dry piece of whole-grain toast, cold coffee, stash yoghurt and spoon in the bookbag along with the essays graded last night, notes for the day's lesson plans, occasionally the rented video of some classic translated to cinema. Water and dry food for the cats. A sigh, perhaps the last breath easily released for the day. To the car, to the high school, to the classroom cage and throwing pearls before the wily beasts.

Her route was short but complex and required a quick jaunt onto the freeway. On Grandlake Boulevard she would catch the freeway on-ramp and exit four ramps north. But this morning she had to pull to a sudden stop. Two new foreign cars behind an older-model Buick were blocking the ramp. A young man in black leather, his white face set off by a vermilion mohawk, bent in an L-shape, elbows and arms resting on the open window of the driver's side. Evidently an amiable conversation, the pedestrian uprighting himself to laugh a few times. One of the drivers in front of Darby honked, and the punk snarled "Fuck you!" menacing with the third finger. Yes, this was the utter breakdown of civilization now. Nobody cared about rules or consideration for others. No police present to enforce the basic traffic rules; each driver, enwombed in his car, fighting through the anarchy on his own.

Best to just wait it out. Don't antagonize the anarchists. They might be armed. People were shot just for passing on the freeway. She'll be late to her first class, but nothing can be done about it. Wait until the driver and his friend give each other the tribal parting cry "Fuck you!" and the Buick revs up onto the freeway to interfere with other people's lives.

Darby had not always believed in civilization. There was a time when youthful rebellion and the impending revolution of 1968 enthralled her. Then she lived more voraciously and uncritically, gorging on love affairs, casual and serious, imbibing the milder, more organic drugs, and espousing most of the political and cultural slogans that wafted in the highly charged ether. In those days she believed in the overthrow of the established culture and its institutions. She became a teacher with the intent of liberating the underclass from its enslavement by the oppressors; she was an inflammatory advocate of literary and intellectual revolution. Much as she loved classics, she believed that they were irrelevant to the lives of her oppressed students, and so she smuggled contraband into the curriculum: books about oppression written by the articulate oppressed. Stories of suffering and heroism. Naturalistic tales in which the individual was prey to the dialectic forces of colonialism, racism, and economic exploitation. Her oppressed students found it depressing.

Something happened to her on the way to the revolution. It started when she noticed that her love affairs had become tedious and redundant, like eating the same food every day. Popular literature and self-help books proclaimed love a disease and she discovered a diagnosis for her inept forays into the jungle of love—obsessive. Darby had to examine her propensity for "wounded" men, her inclination to "love too much" and to be a "co-dependent," and, finally, to acknowledge that she just wasn't very good at selecting romantic leads for her life drama. Her affairs and marriages had been tumultous and passionate, her need to be loved insatiable. Hammond, her first husband, was insufferably selfish and opportunistic. He was an art historian who used his connections in the monied society in which he bowed and scraped to move from one feathered nest to an even more richly-plumaged one. Darby's nest was made of twigs and dew. A few years ago she had seen a photo of him in a New Age magazine. He was dressed in a richly woven serape, wore feathers in his long, unkempt hair, and was the subject of an interview on the spiritual benefits of colonics. He was now on his fourth marriage; an heiress to some military-industrial fortune had dragged him off to a rustic aerie in British Columbia, where she established herself as a neo-Native American shamaness, specializing in cures for truculent bowels, as well as the channeling of some thousand-year-old Inca witch doctor, and had installed Hammond as her factotum, master of ceremonies and lieutenant shaman.

Darby foreswore men after Ty, her last lover, threw up his bellyful of rum on her while they were making love. He moved out and into the arms of yet another "enabler" the very night they split up. It was a final insult to whatever yearnings for happiness in love remained. She began to realize that everyone was really interchangeable in most romances, that Sleeping Beauty could just as well have consorted with the Seven Dwarfs as Snow White, that only names and insubstantial features distinguished Grumpy from Sleepy, and that the love stories she told herself were really all about her. She embarked on forging a solitary new life. Men gradually smelled the sour odor of indifference in her and stopped making approaches. It was a lonely life, but saner than before.

And the oppressed changed too. From the brave marches for equal rights they gained a token middle class and a burgeoning underclass of unemployed. Decaying ghettos and barrios belied the dreams of Martin Luther King, Jr., and Cesar Chavez, while many found that only drugs allowed them to dream their way out of condemned lives. Engaged in the equal-opportunity capitalism of drug dealing, young warlords led their entrepreneurial armies in lethal clashes in the night. Holding their communities hostage, they taunted the powers of the state, daring it to control and contain the violent disorder that bordered and encircled the havens of the privileged classes. The state built more prisons, crammed them with the young troops of this rival military nation-within-a-nation, turned America into a secret prisoner-of-war camp. Undaunted, the young mocked the values imposed by the oppressor, idolized the warlords as resistance fighters, and adopted a street morality that embraced money, murder, and misogyny. Darby floundered between the two camps, abhorring the violence and cruelty of both. She retreated to a traditional paradigm: order and structure and shared values make the world safe. She missed the coziness of civilization.

At school she saw the bundle of memos filling her mailbox, the different-colored papers that greased the clunky, gasping wheels of this nearly toppled institution and generated the lunchroom conversations full of cynicism and spite. Teachers suspected administrators of malfeasance and incompetence; administrators saw a lean and hungry look of conspiracy in the teachers; and parents were convinced that both groups wallowed in the trough of public taxes. On most days Darby avoided the pervasive negativity and backbiting in the English Department lunchroom and ate at her own desk. This, of course, served to isolate her even more from her colleagues, most of whom were two to three decades younger. Many of her peers had already retired or died. Only her inadequate finances kept her at the chalkboard, for she had started teaching late in her thirties and had been profligate with her meager income. But no one really planned to live on the paltry teachers' pensions.

The successfully retired had also been successfully married, with the affluence and security of a two-income family. She had exited her two torturous marriages like a cavalier—without a dime from either man.

"Hey, Darby, did you read Hemlock's memo? Now he wants us to wear badges. I'm not a frigging jail cop. I am a teacher and they barely pay me enough for doing that!" Pierce Grubby had initiated the day with his usual outburst against the injustice of it all. He blocked her access to her cubbyhole, flailing his sheaf of memos, bulletins, and attendance sheets as if they were a banner of insurrection. Pierce's anger was always at the surface and his imposing size compounded the impression that he would fall upon the nearest bystander in a mortal assault. Yet, he was young and handsome in a Teutonic way, and given to witticism, punning, and too-easy smiles, traits that endeared him to the staff and students when his anger abated. He handed Darby the incendiary memo.

To all staff
From Principal John Oswald Hemlock
April 14, 1994

In the past three months we have recorded an increase in the number of assaults on faculty. This unfortunate spate of violence has interrupted the fall semester by creating disruptions to the educational process. Several teachers have taken medical leaves of absence, thereby creating discontinuations in the quality of education for their students.

A number of these incidents have occurred while serving hall duty. We believe that further assaults can be averted if teachers identify themselves and approach the students in the halls in a respectful manner. To that end, we are initiating a program in which teachers will wear badges with their photo and name. These badges must be worn at all times during the school day, or *disciplinary action will be taken.* In addition, we will present a program of role-playing on how to respectfully approach a student at our faculty meeting next Wednesday.

Report to the auditorium Friday at lunch to have your identification photo taken. The badges will be ready and in your boxes by next Monday.

We regret that Karen Ledbetter is still on medical leave for her broken arm, and that Susan Greenberg will not be returning in the Fall semester as she does not expect to fully recover from the spine injury she received when she was shoved down the stairwell last October. We are pleased to announce that Larry Kleindock has recovered from his knife wound and will return for the rest of the Spring semester.

Darby burst out laughing. "If God wanted teachers to defend civilization, he would have given us Gatling guns, not pieces of chalk," she joked to Pierce. But bitterly she thought it typical of Hemlock to reach for this desperate and absurd solution of making the teachers responsible for their victimization. Authority was floundering, the gates were crashing, and, like the Trojan women, she was waiting to see which barbarian would take her life. But there was nothing to do for it.

The morning passed normally with its *tableau vivant* of

sleepy adolescents, occasional moments of intelligent discourse, interruptions by messengers from the office, the counselors, or the health center, mothers looking for the teacher down the hall, a vagrant student trying to catch the attention of a friend. Smothered in this jelly of events, Darby employed Socratic methods, cooperative-learning strategies, sometimes sheer vaudeville routines to arouse the interest of the students. She hoped that one or, God willing, two students might have felt a thrill at a line from *Macbeth*, or suddenly realized that Huck was in love with Jim's humanity, or quivered at the "plague of robins" that accompanied Sula. Whenever she came to it, Darby shivered with empathy at Macbeth's "My life has grown sere" soliloquy, a bleak acknowledgment that this once decent and vital man had come to the end of his life not as a man should, but as something withered, alone, and bestial. But the students performed as they were accustomed, with facility or difficulty, and always with emotional absence. Darby was reminded of Dante's lines:

> We were still standing by the sea's new day
> like travelers pondering the road ahead
> who send their souls on while their bones delay.

Where were their souls—these young souls who sought pleasure in old vices? How many of them would find a passion so scorching that their lives would burn like a lighthouse torch? Who among them would be filled with a spiritual grace that would touch all he encountered? Who would lead masses to a better world? Who would redeem civilization?

Lunch finally came and provided some respite from

the incessant interaction with others. Darby gulped her yoghurt, pulled a Power Bar from the secret stash in her desk, and perfunctorily graded some essays. Fifteen minutes remained before the next class. Best to relieve her bladder; there would be no time later. She headed to the faculty restroom, recently converted from faculty women to faculty unisex, a jarring turn for her celibate sensiblities. However, only teachers had keys to it, so the horrors of the student restrooms could be avoided. But it was occupied, and her need to relieve herself was reaching a critical point. There was nothing to do but head for the girls' bathroom down the hall.

It reeked of urine and shit. Toilets had overflowed. If the school had supplied toilet paper, the kids would not have used the rough ochre paper towels to wipe their behinds and the toilets would not be stuffed up. Darby looked for a stall that still had a door and was not running over with filth. Of the five stalls, only the third bore a half-door and looked as if the toilet could flush. She entered and started to relieve herself. Graffiti covered the walls and door: Tammy loves Chris; Ayisha is a hoe; Bettina is a fuckin bitch; womyn should love womyn; I love myself in my lover-woman's body. And then a long response to the anonymous lesbian :

> You ugly face butt don't know how
> good it is to have him stick his dick in you
> and then turn you over in his hands and do
> it from behind. You are too ugly face to have
> it, so you need ugly face butts like you.
> You'll rot in hell, you bitch.

Darby was surprised at the eroticism of this vituperative wench. Normally, she did not find eroticism stirring, but this crude description of some girl's turn with a worthy stud evoked a few hot memories of passion and lust. Nights with Richard when she could not contain her itch, or Frank's welcome preference for cunnilingus. Better to forget all that. She left it all for the young barbarians now.

She returned to her classroom, sat at her desk, and leaned back in her ancient high-backed chair. It was peaceful there without the energies of the kids zapping pell-mell throughout the room, lightning storms and whirlwinds emanating from each young spirit. Sometimes she thought she could actually see the zigzag bolts and eddying auras flying over the tops of the students' heads, randomly colliding, falling, rising again to clash against another spirit emanence. It was as if each kid had some force that he could not contain, a volatile ether that escaped and became a projectile in search of a target. But it was peaceful now. The long high windows let in the afternoon sunshine. She could see two puffy white cumulus clouds swiftly moving across the blue sky. The room looked light and inviting. She had posters of artworks, portraits of writers, and student art taped to every available surface, and their colors added a vibrant touch to the room.

She was jarred from her complacency by the sound of a mob. She ran to the window. In the courtyard below, a hundred or more kids had circled two fighting boys. As had become the recent custom, the pugilists were bare from the waist up. Both had incredibly broad shoulders, and the taller one had a wasp waist. They were like two beautiful dancers met in combat, but she couldn't see their faces. It was a fierce fight. The boys were striking each other with rapid, powerful jabs. One was knocked off balance, staggered back and tried to restore himself by creating distance from his adversary. But the boy with the advantage moved just as quickly to the retreating opponent and resumed the punching. The crowd backed up and swerved with the fighters, always maintaining that magic circle in which primal life was occurring. They were like a flock of starlings, shifting with the headwinds, changing formation in a flawless mutation of shape. She saw Berle and Jamel, two of the security monitors, plunge through the thick choral mass. Each grabbed a fighter from behind, bending the boys' arms behind their backs. The crowd hissed its disappointment that its bloodlust would not be fulfilled. Several teachers and administrators converged on the excited audience, shooing them off to classes. The fifth-period bell had rung.

The kids straggled in late from the courtyard, still talking about the fight. Undersized scientist-in-vitro Marshall rushed in breathless. "Did you see Lamont, Miz Tangrey? He whipped Ali Williams. Did you see the fight?"

"He whopped his ass," clarified Shantelle Taylor, the pretty little girl who flirted outrageously with Lamont. "Lamont do know how to take care of shit."

"What were they fighting over?" Darby asked.

"Lamont disrepect Ali."

"What do you mean disrespect? What did Lamont say or do to Ali?"

Shantelle inflated with importance as she revealed the motives for the spectacular fight. "Ali be bothern'

Lamont, he be want'n' him to join his posse, be his pawtna. But Lamont say no, he can't break parole. So Ali and his posse say they gonna jump Lamont, but he call Ali out and they start to fight right in the courtyard. You see it, Miz Tangrey?"

"Yes, I saw it." And good for Lamont! she thought. Yet, he had resorted to fighting to defend his integrity. Darby thought she might use this fight to initiate a discussion on violence. Perhaps she might be able to get them thinking about averting fights. But she knew that she couldn't combat the prohibition against being "disrepected." It had become a taboo that, when breached, must be cleansed by ritual violence. She had learned that almost anything could constitute disrespect: an inadvertent brush in the hallway, a failure to keep to established turf in the courtyard. Each ethnic group and class had staked out territories on the cement-topped quarter acre. A student accused Darby of disrespecting him when she told him to be quiet. Disrespect was cause for violence and the rules were amorphous. You waded in the social muck at your own risk.

She saw Lamont later when she was on hall duty. He came to ask for his homework. The ugly purple swelling around his right eye did not mar the mirth and tenderness expressed in those soft brown globes. He was jaunty for someone who had recently fought. Darby was concerned that Lamont would be sent back to juvenile hall for this fight.

"What is the principal going to do to you, Lamont?"

"He suspended me for two days. Tha's all. But Ali got suspended for five days," Lamont cheerfully related.

It was one of the few times in his short life that the establishment had vindicated him.

"Are you worried about repercussions?"

"What's them?"

"I mean, are you worried about the suspension affecting your parole?"

"Nah! The principal knows Ali was pushing me. He said he'll talk to my P.O."

"Well, if you need me to write a letter or testify on your behalf, I will gladly do so." Darby did not want Lamont back in the penal system. He had too much potential. He might turn out to be the last guard at the gates of civilization.

"Finish reading chapters fourteen and fifteen of *Brave New World* and write your responses in your journal. We're going to have a vocabulary test on Friday, so study for it. And, Lamont, I just want to say that I admire you for standing up to Ali, but there are solutions other than fighting."

"Now Miz Tangrey, you don't know what it is to be a man, a black man. You might be able to sweet-talk and jive your way out of shit, but you're a white woman. Bein' white means you don't have to prove yourself to no one. Nobody has whips and guns at your back. So don't judge me, and don't try to color me white!" Lamont's mouth twisted angrily, and for the first time she noticed that his bottom lip was cut and swollen.

Darby didn't think this was the time to argue the safety of white women versus that of black men. Let it go. Lamont might learn later that few people escape the ravages of society. "Okay, Malcolm, just take good care of yourself and do the homework, in case it comes in handy for the revolution." That was her way with him, slight teasing and soft urgings about his aspirations. But she believed in him, even more than he believed in his own glorious future.

The last two classes of the day were uneventful. Darby was always exhausted at the end of the day; it was as if she had been submerged in a tidal wave and could only come up for air after the last student had dropped his gum wrapper on the floor and left. She started sorting the piles of papers on her desk, evaluating which ones she would have the energy to correct this evening. She eliminated the essays on *The Tempest*—too much work for a midweek night. She stuffed some journals and poems into her bookbag, light reading that did not require the copyediting and criticism that essays needed. She removed her purse from the locked file cabinet and started toward the door but stopped short when she heard a girl screaming in the courtyard.

Through the window she could see a circle of boys, perhaps six or seven, and a girl bent over, clutching her stomach and screaming. It was Shantelle. One of the boys was kneeling on the ground, his arm rising and falling in the air. She saw the glint of a knife blade pointed downward, rising and falling, stabbing and gouging.

She ran to the intercom, knowing that it had never worked since it was installed, but praying for a miracle, a fluke. It didn't work. She ran out into the hall. Nobody was on duty.

She tried to get into Pierce Grubby's room to enlist his help, but he had locked his room.

"Sonuvabitch! Open up! I need help!" She was

screaming at the door, pounding it. Pierce did not respond. She ran across the hall to Lucas White's room, but saw a note on the door directing his seventh period to meet in the library. She knew that the other teachers along the corridor would not come out to the courtyard to break up a fight. She abandoned the idea of finding help and ran outside.

She didn't know how much time had elapsed since she'd seen Shantelle and the boys, but when she arrived there was only Shantelle, lying on her side on the ground, moaning and cradling her spilled intestines in the crook of her right arm. Blood pooled on the dirty cement, forming a small red pond between Shantelle and the body of a boy lying with his arms askew, one knee bent up, the other leg thrust out and pointed toward Shantelle. Blood soaked his shirt and pants. Raw flesh jutted from the holes in his chest and throat and groin. She knew, even though his face had been mutilated, she knew it was Lamont.

Darby sat down in the blood next to Shantelle and put her hand on the girl's shoulder. She felt the blood soaking into her own clothes, warm and sticky. She held onto Shantelle, who never stopped moaning, and stared at Lamont's slashed face. It was unrecognizable, that beautiful child's face of her nightmares. She turned to look up at the classroom windows. "Help!" she wanted to scream, but nothing would come out of her throat. She felt her breath stopped in her chest, pressing against her ribs like expanding concrete. Her head dropped to her chin and the hot tears washed down her cheeks, tears so hot they seared her face, filled her mouth with flame, stopped up her throat with lava, a river of steaming tears that ran down to join the warm pond of young blood.

Guardian Angel

Boschka Layton

"Hello?"

My bare feet felt cold on the sloping kitchen floor. The telephone sat on the Goodwill chair-seat at my knees, puffed up like a black genie, on its thin, lumpy, velvet cushion, its slippery length of black snake curling its way up to my ear. I pulled at the snake a bit. It seemed to have a life of its own, winding around down there in the dark. A cold wind swept across the floor; the stripping had come untacked on the bottom of the front door a few feet from where I stood. The last piece of firewood had burnt to a thin red sliver, on a little pile of ash, in the open stove. My bed lay suddenly deserted in the next room, covers thrown back, still warm, waiting for my quick return. Moonlight came streaming in: cold as light.

"Hello."

The voice at the end of the long black coil came through husky, grating, precise; close and warm. It had been a couple of months.

"I just wanted to see if you were there. I've been playing in Guerneville and I thought I might come around to check you out, if you were there. You going to be there?"

"Yes . . . all right . . . so long."

"I'll be there soon . . . so long."

Shit . . . shit . . .

The clock above the telephone, its wan face held together with adhesive tape, said twelve-thirty. Shit.

I felt my way past the stove, got back into bed; pulled the heavy mound of covers up and close till only a few gray tousled lengths of hair showed on the pillows, out of my brown cocoon.

Chances were, he wouldn't show up. Three-quarters of me hoped he wouldn't. Just a god-damned nuisance.

I wondered about the other quarter. That part of myself was generally hard to get at. Pry and pry, and still you didn't really know, or had half-answers. For years, sex had been dormant for me, more or less. Happily quiescent. I didn't really care, had stopped looking. Had already given over. Well, almost a couple of years, anyway. Then this quick brush with it, with this man. Standing looking at each other, half turned away. He'd said something about "the Inn of the Beginning to-night." I had gone on, hadn't thought about it again. I saw him two or three other times, looking at me, over the other heads. Had seen him, one day, putting his hands playfully, jokingly, down inside the Indian shirt of a younger girl I knew, from one of my classes. I had walked silently, abruptly, away. I didn't want any of *that.* God. Enough, at last enough. No more of those jealous twinges and pangs. Enough.

Then one day he came and sat down beside me at lunch. I was matter-of-fact, busy, checking over a paper. He had a little pile of books with him. He put them down between us, on the table; I moved my things away, to make room. His eyes snaked a little, under the lids. He began to talk. He talked for, it must have been, half an hour, fairly low, and serious. Mostly about his life, in the ghetto, in jail. Said his age, forty-eight; that he'd been on heroin until a year ago. It seemed like he'd never talked before and that, once done, he would close up, never have a chance to talk again. I remembered what he'd said about me, that he thought it was time I "got connected" again. I'd said I had had enough of men, they were of a different race of beings. I didn't feel like putting out any more. We sat quietly, and talked. To me it seemed real, and strange, this almost stranger coming up to me, getting me to say things I thought never to say to any man. A solid, sturdy beginning. He had called me ten days later, had come over, had not gone home that night.

I reached out and pulled the pillows around under my head, let my head fall on the other cheek; felt my breasts warm and squashy under me; my weight stretched the length of the bed, toes warm now down there. Still no answers from that other quarter. I put my nose down in the covers, down in that warm breast-y smell. If I could only get a little sleep before he came. I had a lot to do tomorrow. I thought about tomorrow. I hoped he wouldn't stay. Sometimes he did. Went over his lessons. Complained about the eggs. His long body too big for my little house. The comfort of seeing him hunched over, standing in the bathroom, beside the old iron bathtub, washing his penis carefully. I had found an old faded washcloth, he'd demanded one, and it hung on the tap still, stiff with waiting, since the last time. Almost like husband and wife.

Finally, I fell asleep.

I heard him come in. Heard his boots cross the creaky kitchen floor; felt him stoop for the bedroom door and stand there beside the bed, long fingers unbuttoning the stiff leather jacket. I didn't say anything. Then he was down to white singlet and reaching for me under the covers, pulling his long body in beside me. I made a little stirring, mewing sound, still lying with my face in the pillows; willing to let him move me over to his chest, his long arms holding me tight. And I let go, might as well, because it felt so good, his long, familiar, bony body under mine, and lay there on his chest, feeling perfectly at peace, hearing his heartbeat making too much noise in the bent cave of his chest. He seemed subdued, more than usual, still with that eagle presence; the stranger, under the familiar black cap of skull, the small ruby in the tiny ear. He looked down his chest at me, showing his covered snake eyes, his lips thin and fumbling, tight. I missed you sometimes, he said. And tightened his arms against me, stirred his hips; his thin, dear, nonexistent hips. I felt his fingers on the taut skin between my legs, pressing, finding the way in. I helped him a bit with his limp cock: unsure of itself. Oh damn, was it going to be like that, after all? Kissing his neck, his ear. Then it sank in—oh, god, thank god—I made little sexual, happy sounds, pure and sweet, enclosing him with my cunt; heard his answering pure, delighted cries; two mocking birds: he was mine, I loved him: we touched solid length of cheek: clutched arms and legs and bodies: were one, there in the dark, on the white and wrinkled pillows, in the moonlight. Careless of covers.

We lay together on the edge of sleep; rocking with

the waves on the shore, the little waves that make no disturbance; in the green light of the sea. Far and away over the edge of the world we were taken; past soft-limned sea castles; past caves of darker green; past green distances. And brought back to beach against the sand after a long lifetime of hours, in slow ripples of light.

The moon had gone out now. Dark, silent shapes of door and bed hid in the dry cave of room. I had watched two fly-lovers, one hopelessly caught among the fly dead, embedded thickly on the sticky, yellow flypaper, that hung from my kitchen ceiling last summer. He, frantically, hopelessly, pulling at her fragile wings. Their tiny complaints could be heard in the stillness, the stillness of that common grave. His foot had slipped, then one of his wings got caught. Their two siren calls for help had sounded up there, near the ceiling, for a long time. Then they stopped. They were quiet and dead. The flypaper still stirred, reproachfully.

"I've got to get the car back tonight."

He didn't move.

"I borrowed it. I told him I'd bring it back."

He moved his arm a little, under me.

"If I could locate two dollars for some gas, then I could come back tonight."

"I don't have it . . . . You know I don't have it." From the pillows.

He moved unwillingly. Got to a sitting position; the bed made complaining noises. Silently he began pulling on his pants.

"Can't you stay? Do you have to go?"

"I told him I'd bring his car back. . . . He said I could have it longer, if I put some gas in it."

Standing now, his long fingers making a cuff around his seaman's knit cap, close to his head, in the dark.

He walked out and into the bathroom . . . . I heard the long forced rush of water as he peed, heard the wooden beads of the curtain at the toilet door go clank.

He came back, buttoning his fly cautiously, not sure if he could be seen.

He came beside the bed, for a minute, and bent over.

"I might be fortunate and get two dollars for gas, and be back tonight."

I turned and half raised myself to kiss the proffered, tight mouth.

I waited until the front door closed behind him. Heard the car start. Then I threw back the covers and went out to the bathroom and squatted on the toilet. It was a long pee, a long fart hissed out with it, surprised me. I pulled down a few lengths of toilet paper and mopped up the sea-slime of pee and sperm from between my legs. I went back to bed and to sleep, all questions answered. I smiled, going over in my mind his last words "might be fortunate . . ." Smiling. It was always the same: I knew he wouldn't be back tonight. I settled myself to comfortable sleep, the smile still on my face. The covers pulled up around my chin. Cherubim and seraphim, falling down before thee . . . their soft gray wings moving in the light of morning . . . and peace attend thee . . . all . . . through . . . the night.

Wind-chimes, Ivan

Life has so many faces
death
has only one

The wind has flung the wind-chimes against the door.
I wonder if Ivan has found a place to hide.
Then I see him
his cat's whiskers low
white-blown fur on his neck under the black-widow eyes
long drawn out fiddle-head of tail
he wants in.
I take him on my knee, push the papers, books, back, the pen
he is grateful, no claws: ducks under my sweater, my
    hanging scarf-ends
warm in my arm-pit, close as he can get
to the breast.
I circle him
we rock
the breath swells our bodies as one.

Death has so many faces
    life
        has only one.

"Krishna Flossing"
— Boschka Layton

Is There Hope For The Future Cry the Loud Bells of Palsy

I don't reel when I think about my face.
When I see someone reeling not able to look at me
I go home and stare in the looking-glass.
Ah. I see. It's the red and sagging eyeball
that dismays them; the mouth has come
unstuck in one corner.

I forget myself and smile ingloriously at a two-year-old:
he becomes green about the gills suddenly sea-sick for mother.
A friend of twenty years admits she's not used to it.
I tell her look at my best side:
she asks, which is your best side?
On the other hand I haven't been fucked in three years:
you get tired of doing it with your face behind a pillow.
When I worked at the Emporium old ladies would wink back at me;
the butcher in our block used to wink at me, covertly.
He thought I was leading him on.
I thought he was leading me on.

Now local hoods call me scarface.
Bold young cocks give me credit for nothing but senility.
Heckle me when I back in to parallel park: laugh
fiendishly as I lock fenders, pull my steering wheel up by its roots.

If I don't survive the next San Francisco earthquake
don't live to see the second coming of Christ in two thousand and twenty
I may be remembered for a line in Layton's poem to his third wife.

Twenty-four Hour Performance

They each squirm out to center stage:
the spot-light finds
them: my brother on his Streicher frame;
Leslie—tumor of the brain; my mother
brittle with t.b.;
and Gakey—all love in her.

Now it's my turn to be the star.
Wheel me out (let the applause begin)
Crank up the bed—I want *two* pillows—

the better to see
that audience out there
for the last time.

Afternoon In The Sun

I want to be published.
Beside Plath, Philip Roth
the other Layton
howl in red and black
glossy

I stand looking
at that great picture on the wall
the long clapboard side of the house
the long grass, long afternoon sun
some sprawling some sitting
arms on knees
to be taken.
Mother, Dad; Dot & Bill;
Lou Isner—I remember the name
I can't remember him;
the two children squat, hunch
at the feet of the elders:
John peeps wrinkled face behind Les's shoulder.
They are all dead now
except my father: I don't know about Isner
dead too perhaps.
My father's rough long tweed leg cut off
below the calf, at the picture-edge; shirt
sleeve, buttoned at the cuff, leaning against Mother's knees:
they've been bowled over, every one
like the roly-poly clown we knocked about:
bounce back on the wall.

On my table the books are lined up
Plath, Layton, Roth; Lawrence, T.E. & D.H.
Isherwood & Lowry; Olson; Becket.
Slim pickings
after all:
who'd trade them for that afternoon in the sun?

– Boschka Layton

Cathy — Thanks for supporting us, Enjoy the read, Karen Eberhardt

A Woman's Worth

(Why I Am a Poet)

Karen Eberhardt

To my amazement, I am one of the many millions making a home here on this ripe old valiant earth. How small I am, the little sow bug under the loose brick. But not entirely so. If home helps shape the heart, I am very fortunate to live not in a Cairo warren or Delhi maze, not stuck in a Bombay brothel or hidden beneath the veil in Afghanistan, but instead airily situated on a rich and sunny hillside in the drifting fog and golden heat of northern California where there is enough water and land to accommodate my family, sheep, chickens and many wild things.

I am the product of a Unitarian father, a Quaker mother, and by god, this counts for something. These two dear people have often proved to be a burden—they get so caught up in their values and are pulsating with all that intelligence and compassion. But they raised me to think twice about what I do with my life, for which I thank them, and it is to their credit I have done nothing *but* reflect on who I am, where I am going, whether I strive to live up to their visionary ideals, even though they lost control when I was about seventeen. Fortunately, some good things stick and there are no rules or formulas for why this happens. The pendulum could have swung the other way—I might have been a hostess in Las Vegas, a drug addict on the streets.

But no, in my teens, hot passion turned me into Joan of Arc, Florence Nightingale, anything I dreamed of. I soaked up their altruism and moral fiber, and started turning it into poetry at an early age. I simply became a poet and that is what I have stayed. Through marriage, travel, travail, an adopted daughter from India, dead sheep in the barnyard, Vietnam, Nixon, Reagan, divorce, deep financial stress, Chernobyl, the fall of the Berlin Wall, the war in Yugoslavia, and the long upheaval of a passionate love affair that left me lonely but independent, I cranked out those little poems, the hiccups of my heart.

I marched against bomb tests and nuclear power plants, visited prisoners in jail (without asking why they were there), and spoke out on the inherent rights of mosquitoes before deep ecology became a movement. In the process, I discovered my voice. Yes, I am passionate about the planet—our beautiful precocious child flitting around among all the old patriarchs in space—but could easily have gone mad among a surfeit of issues. The waste and cruelty, ignorance and greed. After a time, you realize all this is so, that your fragile sphere of influence can reach only so far, and then what?

I began to write with serious intent. Poets don't change the world, but ultimately true poets will not be censored, edited or deflected from putting heaven and hell into words. They maintain a certain influence amongst the many tests that help decide our human fate. They stand somewhat apart from the ordinariness of everyday life—stirring little pots, weaving webs, peering into crystal balls, like oracles on the skyline pointing at all the conflicting, and often destructive, directions we choose to take.

I once visited Mother Teresa in Calcutta and wanted to be like her. I saw her as one of those beings who do great things, set others before themselves, devote their lives to healing and restoration. They represent the cream of humanity, and we can never be thankful enough for their single-minded devotion to their tasks. But I didn't have the qualities to become a saint, a mountain climber, a ballerina or violinist, a politician or Third World doctor. I stayed a poet, directed by a creative will whose mysterious influences I will never fully fathom.

Now I am what is called a mature woman and there's not much room left to have illusions about who I am or what I'm doing with my allotted years. I'm a poet, and while that's not the whole picture, it pretty well sums it up. I care less about being a significant person doing good in societal or community terms, and more about listening to my solitary core, following its dictates, finding a way and making time to be the best poet it is in me to be. That is what it finally comes down to: striving, giving form to, opening up the voice, vibrating against one's self, which in turn vibrates against the dust motes of the universe, the chlorophyll in grass, the enormous, enigmatic, vibrant, astounding spirit animating the entire planet and all the tiny, steady miracles taking place right outside the door. I'm more or less content to live with that. I've found my voice. I see with acceptance that it's who I am. To take what you've become and use it as a tool for good, for love, for whatever works . . . can there be any higher goal?

A Country Life

I will not be defined as just one thing;
I also live on a farm. I am a country woman.
I flex limbs in oilskins and rubber boots
during downpours to care for chickens and sheep.
Mud coats everything I touch and has its own taste
along with sodden mulch, the warm shit of animals.
I am comfortable with this messy natural state
where the wet drumming follows in the harness
allowing each part its dance of hooves and roots.
This is not my whole routine but it runs through
everything I do, pinning me down practically
to the way days and nights and weather
deal with feathers and fleece, the cats and mice
in the straw, the economics of sparrows
foraging with chickens for cracked corn.
I am linked to fences and the barn,
the turning of worms after heavy rains,
the syncopation of wind and sun and seeds
breaking open their skins in time for the end
of the heavy frosts, ice in the hoses and pipes;
our train of thought remarkably alike
whether we are duck or sheep, woman out in rain
holding it together out of love, a shared life,
and her own need, like theirs, to endure
on this burgeoning and fecund skin of earth.

Ducks

I love ducks.
I love the way their necks
curl above the grass
and when they run their feet splat
and rock their cylinders from side to side
like small boats
hurtling through waves.
Home to them is where they go last
following hens and sheep
back to where they sleep.
I love their beaks
guzzling in mud,
mates until the last pair of them
sees their dark way back
after light has fallen
off their backs.
I love ducks' wise ways
their very duckness
one smooth feather lined with down,
their quack a lack of artiface.

Man's Sunday

I was Maid of the Morning doing it all
out of responsibility instilled from the beginning
I walked down the long drive for the Sunday paper
fed the animals, made sure the fire burned hot
stood in the doorway with two mugs of tea.
I earned my brief share of your warm body in bed
while working my way through the funnies
and a few minutes of serious reading.
Then it was time to make omelettes, toast the bagels
and switch to coffee for late breakfast instead
of being still, doing nothing, thinking.
You turned on the radio for one game, tv for the other
just like my solid old husband used to do.
I watched the rain spoiling it for families
on the green hillside trying to cut Christmas trees
and sized up my sense of bondage,
the age-old futility of exercising female choice
on a wet Sunday when I could use these soft hours
to surrender to my self instead
of the roar of football as it fills my ears
this cultural model too hard to erase in one day
your intentness on following your team
supercedes my longings; I merely follow
the rain, understanding how it is
but somehow resenting it
because so rarely is there any choice.
You would be mystified if I intervened,
which I wouldn't because I understand these things
even though my heart revolts.

One Is Good, Two Is Better

I want somebody to be there,
just be there like my shoes
in piles under the shelf waiting for me
to step into them. When sleep abandons me
at 3 am, I watch the moon's silent glide
through the clear ice of space
and fear that light.
But if your warm bones would gather up my body
someone normalizing half the bed
whoever you are, the demons would let me
go by, the bulk of you a password
holding off the sad distance
the crackling static of a heartbeat
that dog's muffled melancholy whine.
If you would just be there
like the same comforter every night
surrounding me with a fence
of gentle breathing, a fortress
of dependable flesh, your own flannel-lined
dreams, I would love sleeping again,
love slipping away into my unconscious
giving you half my fears, my loneliness,
whoever you are, our lovely pair of shoes.

Easter Lily

There is nothing more beautiful than this Easter lily;
stamen and pistel lying in the creamy mouth,
the white cone holding a hollow of shadow
and radiance filtering through the green membranes.
The whole memorizing three fluted layers of skin
curling like a soft trumpet back into the air,
and three more overlaying them, smaller;
all six together opening the white face;
the alabaster prayer layer upon layer
unfolding serenely toward heaven.

One by one the pale lime pods open;
twelve apostles crowning an apogee of stalks.
Their mouths unfurl in all directions,
nun-like and prayerful, softly gleaming
in this rain drenched light; sisters and virgins
in silent vigil too perfect for human perfidy.
Watching them evolve into holy beacons
smoother than flesh makes me tremble;
there is nothing more beautiful than an Easter lily
in April when my heart longs for all the stones to roll away.

To Cathy Hawkins
Best Regards

Found Money

Ianthe Elizabeth Brautigan

Mary turned the knob on the sprinkler system and stepped out of the water's range. She stood barefoot on the warm concrete and looked at the tract houses down the street, each lawn green with its edges neatly trimmed and the sidewalks swept clean. Instead of turning quickly and going back into the house, as she had done a hundred times before, Mary looked carefully at the street where she had lived for six years. The static stillness of the houses became hypnotic and made her stand very still, almost frozen. I'm becoming a sort of suburban statue, she thought. For a small moment, she could see herself as if from outside her own body, long-legged with short, fine, brown hair, wearing khaki shorts and a faded Peter Frampton T-shirt. What am I doing with my life besides making sure my lawn stays green? Before these unexpected thoughts could continue, Ben touched Mary's shoulder.

"Are you coming in? Evan and Annie want a kiss good night."

She went in and kissed her children. They were full of animated talk, the kind designed to keep sleep away and parents near. Her youngest, Annie, chose this time to tell Mary her dreams because she knew it was the one thing her mother would never cut her short on.

Ben was sitting on the couch that his folks had given them. Its dreary brown Naugahyde upholstery actually gave it character, and she had grown fond of it. Everyone else she knew had matching furniture. Grey-blue seemed to be very popular right now. A couple of times she and Ben had stood in the furniture section in Sears and been tempted to go into debt and match. But they could never make up their minds which couch to buy and so they would give up and go home relieved. Mary told everyone they were waiting until the kids grew up. But, in truth, she wasn't sure they would ever have the courage to actually pick out a couch and then purchase it. Ben, weary from the day, turned on the TV. Mary sighed, went in to do the dinner dishes and found that they were done. She walked back into the living room and kissed the top of Ben's head.

"Thank you," she said. He pulled her down on his lap and leaned against her breasts. "You looked sad," he said, "and dishes aren't good for the blues."

"You know what I want to do?" asked Mary, taking a deep breath.

"Have wild, crazed sex on the clean laundry?"

"No, I want to go on a trip. I want to go to Europe."

"Are you Mary?" asked Ben, lifting up her shirt and looking underneath. "The Mary I married has a hard time taking a trip to San Francisco. My Mary says things like, 'Do you think the coffeemaker's on?' when we go to the movies."

"Stop that. I'm serious. I want to go to Europe."

He pulled his head out from under her shirt. "Who would pay for this trip? What do we tell my boss? And the biggest question is, who would mow our lawn? The lawn police would be after us if we let it go."

"I don't know," she said. Ben settled back on the couch, turned up the sound and said, "Maybe someday."

Mary climbed in bed and read until she fell into a deep sleep, which ended about 3:00 a.m. when she dreamed that the answer to her money problem was aluminum cans, piles and piles of aluminum cans.

It was one of those dreams that made total sense at 3:00 a.m. and absolutely none at 7:30 a.m. when her eight-year-old son was asking her if he could go swimming. Mary shook her head no. "First, I have to make some coffee." Ben was still buried underneath the comforter. She could see a bit of his hair standing up in a comforting way. "Maybe there's something on TV," Mary said to Evan, feeling guilty for sending him to watch TV. She had friends whose children never watched TV, although Mary wasn't sure how people were parents before TV.

She debated whether to tell Ben her plan. Then because it was her habit to tell him everything, she did. He didn't say anything, except that it might take her awhile and to remember to get a sitter for the party on Saturday, please.

Mary got a pair of rubber gloves and a garbage bag from under the sink. She went to all the people on her block and asked if she could collect their cans. Mary took the bag of cans and got cash for them at the recycling center, $5.80 worth. There wasn't a line, and the old man who redeemed her cans was very polite.

They went to the party. She wore a nice dress and they looked like maybe they didn't have kids. The party was at his boss' house, which was very chic. Not only did things match, they were incredibly expensive matching things. Most of the people at the party were professionals and looked like they went to Europe every week or so.

Mary loved parties and people, but there was always a sticky point and that was when people said: So, what do you do? And she said that she had dropped out of college to get married. And then people would say that it seemed she was well educated, And Mary would say she read a lot. And then they would say how they thought what she was doing was important. Or people would say: How can you stay at home? It must be so boring. Or: Why don't you go back to school? Mary had found a fairly good strategy. She would keep the people talking about themselves. But now, she had something to say.

Her husband's boss came by and asked her what she was up to.

"Collecting cans to go to Europe," Mary said.

"Repeat that," he said.

"Collecting aluminum cans so Ben and I can go to Europe," she said.

"Just how do you go about this?" he asked.

"Well," she said, "I have a kind of route in my neighborhood," and then she giggled. "I guess you could say I'm sort of a suburban bag lady. In fact, if I could, I would love to have the cans from this evening. That is, of course, if you recycle."

He looked startled at the insinuation that he might not recycle and excused himself from her, saying, "Of course we recycle; just check with the caterer in the kitchen about the cans."

Before they left she went into the kitchen for the cans. A young girl with heavy eyeliner and bangs teased up at least four inches said, "Sure. They're over there," and pointed to a box. Mary wanted to ask the girl how she got her bangs to stand up that way, but instead she lugged the cans out the back door. Ben had the back of the station wagon open for her.

"Have you figured out how long this will take you, Mary?" he asked.

"I don't know," she said. "I was never any good at math, so I'm just not counting yet."

$17.25. She began not to be so afraid of the winos and the homeless at the recycling center. She sat down with Annie and Evan and Ben and then figured out that at the rate she was going it would take eleven years and three and a half months. There was a silence at the table. "I guess I'll have to expand my route," she said. Evan and Annie thought that was a good idea.

"Over by the school, it seems like people drink a ton of sodas," Evan said.

"Mr. Baxter drinks lots of beer," said Annie, excitedly. "I'll bet you could get about fifty cans a week from him."

Mary opened up a savings account for the trip. The small green passbook the young teller handed her made her feel a little more official. It was at this point that her friend Eloise came over and stood in the driveway watching her load cans to take to the recycling center.

"Mary, people are beginning to talk."

"Why on earth would anybody talk about me?"

Eloise began to squirm and squint her eyes. "It's the

cans. People think it's weird."

Mary looked at Eloise's feet. Her toenails were two-tone. Mary wanted to ask Eloise how she did that, keeping the colors separate, but instead asked, "Why? What's weird about wanting to go to Europe? It's an educational thing."

"It's not that Mary, it's the way. It's this can thing."

"I have tried to think of other ways, but the only job I could get would be at the mini-mart. And, by the time I paid for child care, most of the money would be gone. I thought about cleaning houses, but I hate to clean my own so why would I want to clean anyone else's?" Mary stopped talking because she was about to start yelling and she didn't quite know why. She finished loading the cans, called for her kids and left for the recycling center. Her kids loved to go to the center. Annie could always be counted on to talk to the strangest person there. Evan wanted to take a shopping cart home. "It would be so cool, Mom."

Margaret, one of the homeless women, who also redeemed her cans in the early afternoon, offered Evan and Annie a cookie. They stared at Mary, putting her on the spot. Mary glanced at Margaret. She seemed healthy, and the cookies looked clean. Still Mary wondered what diseases you could possibly get from a cookie that a homeless person gave you. She gave a weak smile and said, "Sure."

She waited for Ben to come home so she could cry.

"What . . . what?" he asked.

"People think I'm weird," she sobbed into his shoulder.

"Who says you're weird?" he asked.

"Eloise."

"The Eloise who has covered all her furniture in plastic and wipes her phones with alcohol after anyone uses them thinks you're weird?"

"It isn't that so much," and Mary wailed. "All that math doesn't lie; the trip will take forever at the rate I'm going."

"Who said Europe would come easy?" he said and kissed her. "You know, you could take the kids to the public pool instead of joining the swim club next summer, and that would be four hundred dollars towards the trip. And I could ask the boss if you could get the cans from work every week."

Ben began to act differently. He began painting again. He had been an art major in college before he had become a layout artist for the local paper. That was how they met. He had tried to paint her picture, but they always ended up making love instead. He had a reputation for screwing the women he painted. Her friends were horrified when she started dating him and even more so when she and Ben got married.

Ben began going to the recycling center because he liked sketching the trees on the hill behind it. The kids were thrilled because they got to spend even more time there. Margaret let Evan push her cart, and Annie played with a skinny, grey cat, which they ended up taking home. It was a relief to Mary to just take the cat. She had been afraid the kids would ask if they could bring Margaret home.

Mary began shopping at the discount food warehouse on the other side of town. Eloise had been upset when she saw Mary unloading the bags. "How can you stand it? The people there are so poor; it's so depressing."

Mary couldn't think of anything to say. Eloise was right. It was a little depressing.

One day she had been shopping behind a group of Hell's Angels. They had tattoos and were wearing leathers, and she was a little nervous about passing them in the aisle. But when she got up close enough to see what they were doing, she found they were looking at soup cans intently, comparing prices. Mary almost laughed out loud with relief.

Even though Mary had far from enough money, she began to prepare for the trip. She wrote to people in London who might want to trade houses for two weeks. She met a college kid who was working at the recycling center for community service because of a drunk driving ticket. He had biked across Europe the summer before. He gave her his maps and the names of the cheap places to stay and eat. Whenever he gave her the money for the cans, he would say, "This one's for breakfast," or "Another dollar for your ticket."

She sat down with Ben and they began planning what they wanted to see. He left it mostly up to her. "It's your trip. The only thing I would like to do is go to some museums," he said. Annie wanted to know all the different ways they would travel. "An airplane and trains," she whispered over and over again reverently. And Evan was happy that he was going to have a backpack. It was almost as good as a shopping cart. They would have a base in London and take a trip to France, even though she heard the French were rude to people.

The next time, she brought plums from her tree for Margaret and the people at the recycling center.

She sat down with the calculator and figured out that, at this rate, she would have enough money to buy the tickets next summer, but it wouldn't be until the following summer that they would be able to go. She began to get discouraged, thinking that it was going to take too long. On TV everything happened in a half an hour. The absolute longest it took to solve a problem was two hours, and that was for the movie of the week.

It was then that she began to dream about her great-grandmother. In the dreams, her great-grandmother was always doing something: scrubbing, canning or weeding. Her great-grandmother didn't have time to talk to her. Even if she had spoken, Mary wouldn't have understood her because her great-grandmother spoke only German. She had lived on a farm homesteaded by her father for sixty years and then the Depression came and her husband died and the farm was lost. All that work for nothing. Everybody moved to California and her great-grandmother finished her life making pickles in her bathtub in Watsonville.

When Mary woke up, she asked Ben if he ever had dreams about his great-grandparents.

"No," he said.

Mary fell silent. The cans, the dreaming and Europe were all taking their toll. She began to feel lightheaded.

"Do you know what my mother said when I told her we were going to Europe?" she asked.

"What?"

"She said I should go to hairdressing school instead."

"What has hairdressing school got to do with Europe?"

"I don't know. Ben, I was thinking. Maybe we

should just forget this Europe thing and buy a new couch or make a down payment on a new car, or I could go to hairdressing school. Eloise says you can get low-interest loans."

"Mary, even the kids won't let you cut their hair, and besides, it's your trip." He walked over and put his hand in his underwear drawer. "I have some money. I haven't been eating out at work and the grand savings is $30.02."

Mary hugged him.

After he left for work, her mother called back. "I've been thinking. Maybe you shouldn't go to hairdressing school. Maybe you should go to business school."

"Mother, have you lost your mind?"

"No. I just watched a Phil Donahue show about mothers who didn't encourage their children, and I wanted to make up for lost time."

"What lost time, Mother?"

"All the time I spent telling you to get married instead of encouraging you to be you."

"Is that what the show was called, Mother?"

"No. The show was mothers who regretted not encouraging their children. *Encouraging You to Be You* is the book I bought. Maybe your sister wants to go to beauty school. I know, I'll send you twenty-five dollars towards your Europe, and that will be—"

"Encouraging me to be me," Mary finished. "Mom, do you think it's weird I collect cans?"

"Of course. Your great-grandmother is probably the only one who wouldn't."

"Why wouldn't she?"

"Because she worked so hard all her life. 'Found money' is what she would have called the cans."

"Mom, why did she come to America?"

"I don't know," she said. And then after a slight pause, "Her name was Emma. She made pickles and sent me quilts on my birthdays."

"I love you, Mother."

"I love you too, baby."

The money began to add up like an old black-and-white movie when it showed time passing on a calendar.

Mary stopped having much to say to her friends. They kept talking about ordinary things, and it seemed like everything she thought about was different now. It was an unsettling feeling. Sometimes she missed the comfort of the way life had been, because now she was always in motion, pushing through time instead of watching it go by, measuring things by outgrown clothes and the holiday bazaars at the church and when the pool closed. She felt like a rodeo rider holding on and the ten-second buzzer wasn't sounding. Ben was painting in the attic, and although Ben remembered to mow the lawn, they didn't plant any flowers. Their house looked plain next to the neighbors'. The old woman on the corner commented on it.

"No flowers," she said.

"No flowers," and Mary added, "in fact, we're thinking of cementing everything over and painting it green." The lady looked startled. "It's just a joke," Mary said hurriedly.

Her mother sent the $25.00 and a card that said, "Go for the gusto. Love Mother."

Her sister, Suzanne, called and wanted to know why Mary hadn't called to warn her about their mother.

"You'd think me being a real estate agent would be enough, but where did she get this beauty school idea?"

"Maybe she just wants you to have a backup career, and besides being a wife, that's all she thinks women can be. Sometimes I wonder if she's right."

"You have two beautiful children and a wonderful husband," her sister said. "Lots of people would like that. Besides, you're going to Europe."

"The problem is that those are not marketable skills. And can collecting doesn't exactly fill out my resume."

"You have to admit it's unique. Great-grandmother Jacobs would have approved; she couldn't stand waste."

Mary's heart started beating hard. "What do you remember about Great-grandmother Jacobs?"

"She was really old and she made pickles in the bathtub."

"Do you ever dream about her?"

"Never. If you're so curious, ask Mom."

"In her current frame of mind, that could be dangerous. I could end up whatever the last Donahue show was."

Suzanne's call-waiting began to click. "Got to go."

Mary began cleaning up the kitchen with the cat meowing at her heels. Toast crumbs and old bowls of cereal were everywhere. The children were gone until after dinner. She thought about grabbing her suit and going to the pool, but she wasn't in the mood to sit with everyone. The only exciting thing that had ever happened at the pool was a fight between two mothers in the shallow end and she had missed it. Evan had told her about it when she picked him up. "Their faces were this close," and he put his nose about a quarter of an inch from hers.

And then he said, "And they were yelling at the top of their lungs."

Instead, she went to the library to check out books on Europe.

"Are you going on a trip?" the librarian asked.

"Yes, I am," she said.

On the way home, she swung by and checked her Thursday can route, $9.80. And when Margaret offered her a cookie, she took a nibble and palmed the rest. A little stale, but she didn't die.

She called Ben at work. "No kids. Bring Chinese food and let's have wild sex in the living room."

"Mary, I have cans," he whispered seductively.

"You're so romantic," Mary said.

She hung up the phone and it rang again. It was Suzanne. "I can't talk, I just want you to guess who's going to beauty school."

"Mom."

"Yes, and Dad is having a you-know-what fit. Call you tonight."

The late afternoon sun shone on the kitchen floor. The cat, which they had named "Fluffy," was curled up under the table looking a little less skinny, but nowhere near fluffy. The linoleum was sticky from lunchtime limeade. Mary looked out the window and felt a sense of joy at everything, a welling up of emotion and freedom that she hadn't felt in a long time. She knew that her dad wouldn't allow her mother to go to beauty school and that no one really believed she was going to Europe except for Ben and the children and her great-grandmother; that is, if people in dreams really counted. She shut the drapes and took her clothes off in the laundry room, starting a load of darks while she was in there. She had to duck down to get out of the kitchen without being seen by the neighbors. This made her feel ridiculous and sexy all at the same time.

Mary heard Ben's car in the driveway and the rattling of the cans as he took them out of the car. The sound, which was so ordinary to most people, was now something very different to her. There seemed to be a place opening up in the air, and if it could hold this sound for her, maybe it could hold something else. She stepped forward and called out into it. "Ben, it's Mary. I'm in the living room."

"Well, Mary, it's Ben. I'm in the garage. Come and help me with the cans." She thought about grabbing her robe, but no one could see her if she went through the kitchen. She had to crawl again, which made her giggle.

"What are you laughing about?" he asked.

"Nothing," she said, laughing more. "Is the garage door shut?"

"Yes. Why?" he asked.

"Open the door and you'll see," she said.

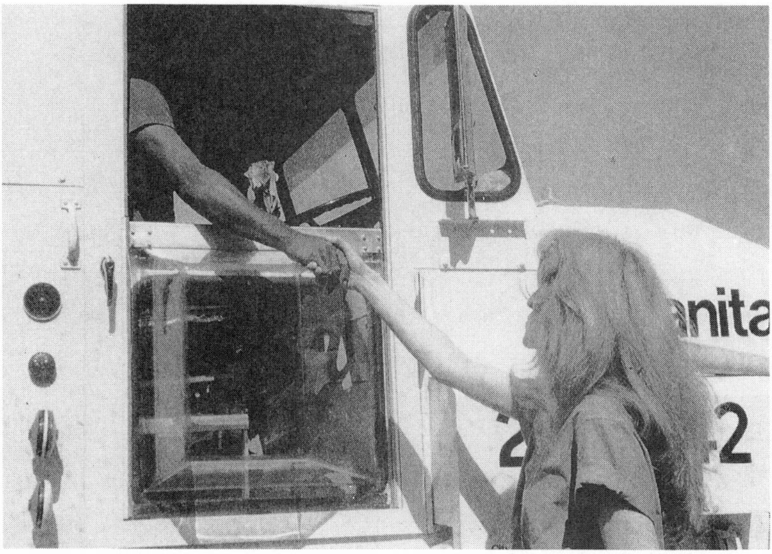

Mierle Laderman Ukeles. Touch Sanitation 1979-81. Courtesy Ronald Feldman Fine Arts. New York

Maintenance Art: Mierle Laderman Ukeles

Karen Petersen

"After the revolution, who's going to pick up the garbage on Monday morning?"

In 1969, Mierle Laderman Ukeles found herself struggling to create art and raise her family. Women artists were rarely housewives; anyone who was took care to hide it when showing her work in the serious art world.

As a wife and mother, Ukeles did "a hell of a lot of

washing, cleaning, cooking, renewing, supporting, preserving. . . . These maintenance everyday things were taking me away from making art." She found that "culture confers lousy status on maintenance." Her brilliant solution to this conflict was to confer art status on her own labors. Her earliest pieces, titled Care, were performing the everyday tasks of caring in public. "I will sweep and wax the floors, dust everything, wash the walls, cook, invite people to eat, clean up, put away, change light bulbs. . . . My working will be the work."

In 1973, Ukeles, mop in hand, took up a post at the Wadsworth Atheneum in Hartford, Connecticut, where she performed Washing, Tracks, Maintenance: Maintenance Art Activity III. As museum visitors passed through the halls, she continued to wash the floors throughout the day, piling up the rags that she used on the site. Determined to bring "maintenance" activities before the public, she proceeded to search out larger public venues for her art.

A Manhattan resident, Ukeles was keenly aware of those who "kept New York City alive" by taking away the trash. In her best-known piece, Touch Sanitation, 1980, she walked the streets of New York with sanitation workers for a year and a half, photographed them and listened to their stories. She personally shook hands and thanked all 8,500 members of the Department of Sanitation. "I hope that my handshakes will eventually burn an image into the public's mind that every time they throw something out, human hands have to take it away."

New York City throws out 26,000 tons of garbage a day. It was not only the sheer immensity of labor that touched Ukeles, but the contempt which the workers were shown by the city's residents. One man told her about picking up garbage in Brooklyn on a hot day. They had taken a break and were sitting on someone's front porch. A woman opened her window and yelled, "Get away from me, you smelly garbage men! I don't want you stinking up my steps." Ukeles responded with a performance piece, Cleansing the Bad Names, wherein she covered the walls of a gallery with the names the workers get called: dirtbag, can man, slimeball, slob, trash hound. "For seventeen years," the worker told Ukeles, "that has stuck in my throat. Today, you cleared it away." On the day of the opening, the assembled group of art commissioners, city officials, artists, company presidents, and sanitation workers were all handed sponges and invited to help clean the graffiti-covered walls.

In what seems a natural progression, Ukeles' focus moved to landfills themselves, and the critical issue of non-degradable waste. In her 1990 exhibit, Garbage Out Front: A New Era of Public Design, she asked: "Can the same inventiveness that we use for production and accumulation of goods be applied to their disposal?" She designed a passage ramp at the Hudson River Transfer Station which permitted visitors to view the dumping operations that daily handle 26,000 tons of garbage. By displaying every part of the process of waste and waste management, Ukeles hoped to inspire a search for new models of consumption and disposal of goods.

"After seeing this, you'll never be able to say your garbage doesn't matter."

LUNA
DIABLO
Dia de Los Muertos
M.L. '96
sugar

Tragafuego

(from the novel Kiss the Ground)

Laura del Fuego

It was summer after my father died that we left Aunt Dede's and took the train from the border at Mexicali through the Sonora desert into Mexico. Mama, my brother Henry, and I. It was dry and windy and hot. "Snake country," Mama said. We were on our way to Tio Rojelio's ranch. We could stay with her uncle for free, Mama said. "We have no money. And I am not going to work in the fields. Ever again." Before the train took off Henry and Mama got into a fight because he insisted on bringing his collection of rock 'n' roll records and his old plastic record player. "It's too heavy," my mother said. "You are not taking it."

"Yes. I am." Henry glared at her.

"No!" she screamed at him.

He stood, eyes glowering, daring her. "I am, and you can't stop me."

She hauled off and whacked him, grabbed him by the neck, slapping him over and over. He just stood there, letting her shake him like a rag doll. "I'm not going." His lip trembled.

"Ay que vivo! Just what do you think you're doing?"

"I'll live in the hills," he said, heading off the train with his sack of records and the beat-up funky record player.

"Come back *here,* Henry! *Cabron* . . . Get back." But he kept on going.

"Okay . . . Okay," she yelled. "Bring it!"

"He would have never dared if your father was here. *Never,"* she said later. "It's his head. The blow on the head." I didn't know if she meant from falling off the horse that day and hitting his head on the rock, or the way he used to bang it on the wall when he was upset.

"Que vamos hacer con el? What are we going to do with him?" she whispered, staring out the window.

Ever since the "accident" that took my father, my mother had changed. She acted as if I weren't there. Her eyes were weird, glazed, her mouth sad and ugly. She hated me. I knew it, and it occurred to me that it was my fault. *My fault that my father had died.* I remembered when they fought. Daddy drunk and mean—scary. I wished—yes—prayed that God would make him stop. Take him away. The day it happened, we were coming back from grocery shopping. Mama had stopped at Aunt Irina's and they had sat at the kitchen table drinking beer and smoking and listening to Lola Beltran on the record player. I kept thinking that Daddy was going to be mad if we got home late again. I could see him grabbing her. I saw Mama push, slap him. Then the yelling. I remember thinking, I wish he was dead!

But later, when I thought about it, it was as if someone else had uttered the words. Some hateful ugly spirit, lurking over my head.

Tio Rojelio had a ranch with a cow, an old burro, and a milk goat. He grew lettuce and squash and tomatoes that he took to market. Morelia was the closest city, thirty miles away. It might as well have been a million. About a mile away was the small town of Cerano with its plaza, its fruit and candy vendors, its dried-up fountain, its bakery with the gigantic oven where we bought bread for a penny, and its dusty tiny shack of a post office. Everything that was important happened in the plaza. In my opinion, after leaving the coast at Aunt Dede's, that was nothing.

Great-aunt Rivera had died. The Indian woman Rocio, who lived on the ranch taking care of the house and doing the cooking, told us that my great-aunt had been hexed by a bruja. She saw the witch, she said, flying on a broom over the barn one dark rainy night.

"Your great-aunt couldn't eat, and got very weak," Mama said. "She had anorexia—she starved. Don't pay attention to that girl. She's superstitious."

Henry sneered, and when Mama was out of earshot said, "Look who's talking."

Right away Rocio took us to the Catholic church to be blessed by the priest. She said she was afraid that the evil spirits that had hexed Aunt Rivera might inflict a similar fate upon us, especially since we were still young and susceptible, and full of crazy foolishness. God knows what we had brought over from El Norte, she said curling her lip distastefully.

We went to the little dried-up town once a week for mass. Rocio gave us frayed pictures of Jesus with His big red heart throbbing and glowing. *"Es safada, esa mujer.* She's goofy," my mother said about Rocio behind her back. But she made us wear the little pictures stuck with safety pins to our underwear. Rocio was always going on about miracles and curses, God, Mary, La Virgen de Guadalupe. But more than anything it was El Diablo she was hot for—the devil and hellfire. The world was going to come to a horrible cataclysmic fiery end one day soon. Very soon. If we weren't careful we were all going to hell, and there we would languish with the demons, the unspeakable creatures that had betrayed Dios Santito. Rocio had a picture in her bedroom of a woman engulfed, consumed in a blaze of phosphorescent orange flames. I'd stare at it, mesmerized by the woman's unshakable faith, her eyes turned upward, her face glowing, beatific in the midst of unimaginable torture and agony.

I thought of Sister Evangelina telling us that just thinking bad thoughts was a sin. I wondered if it was a mortal sin? If you died with it on your soul would you go to hell and burn forever? I took heart from the woman's arduous passion, her passive defiance. I vowed to accept my destiny with courage, a passionate renunciation. Like Joan of Arc—let them burn me. I would die a heroine—a saint. I saw my mother with tears streaming down her face, shattered with remorse and grief.

It was the day after I dreamed about my father that I saw the dead baby. In the dream Daddy was alive. I felt his warm hand holding mine. Rocio had taken us to church. Mama had a headache and had stayed at home. We followed the procession in the wake of a tiny casket surrounded with bouquets of baby breath and pink roses. We walked into the church behind the women with the black shawls and lace mantillas, and got on our knees and prayed to *la Virgen.* Then we followed the people in line past the casket. I saw the tiny, gray body in a white fluffy dress, shriveled and stiff. The women left bowls of rice and candy along with flowers and holy cards on the altar for the dead baby.

I was thinking, is this what my father looked like? Mama wouldn't let me look at him at the funeral. It was as if he had disappeared into thin air. . . .

Later that afternoon Rocio made a lunch and took us to the cemetery for a picnic. We sat with our food spread out amongst the old tombstones, graves, and wilted flowers while she told stories. There was the saint-like nun who had cared for orphans all her life. Her corpse had shrunk to the size of a small child and was buried in the children's cemetery in a tiny habit with miniature rag dolls and pictures of all the children she had cared for at the orphanage to keep her company in heaven. She told us that it was dangerous to be wealthy because it made one have less compassion and end up in mortal danger of losing one's soul. She proceeded to tell the story of the stingy rich man who had come to town and taken his big black horse with the shiny silver stirrups and fancy saddle to the local blacksmith for shoeing. On the road there he had met a sickly woman carrying a baby and begging. He heartlessly ignored them, kicking dust in their faces as he spurred his horse on.

Pero Dios te paga. God will get even! On that dark highway with only the sliver of a new moon, owls hooting, wolves and stray dogs howling, they found him trampled and bloody. His horse had vanished. There he lay wretched and lifeless, an ominous circle of horseshoes around his mutilated body. A sign, Rocio said, crossing herself, *"Era Santo Tomas,"* the patron saint of blacksmiths and the poor, wreaking revenge.

And then there was the time that Father Obregon discovered that the devil was ringing the church bell at midnight, the witching hour, scribbling thirteen on the bell tower with witches' blood. The priest performed an exorcism so powerful it ripped out the devil's tongue, and it flew away as if it had wings and came back at night looking for victims. Everyone in town had to be blessed with holy water and incense. And now during the full moon you could see it, *la lengua del diablo,* the devil's tongue with wings like a bat beating at the window panes. You ran and got a crucifix to flash at it, crossed yourself and prayed to *Madre de Dios Santito.* Rocio said we should never go out at night, especially around the dark of the moon, because the devil, this flying winged tongue, liked children best. Especially light-skinned ones as they were easier to see. She doused us with holy water, marking a tiny cross on each of our foreheads.

One night in early November, Mama draped torn white sheets over our heads, poked holes for eyes and mouths, using charcoal from the wood-burning stove to smudge our faces and draw circles around the eyeholes. We were getting ready to go out for El Dia de los Muertos. Rocio wore a black shroud, and donned a papier-mâché mask of a skull. Henry said it was like Halloween. But Mama said it wasn't, because we were going to pay our respects to the deceased. In Mexico people thought of it as a holy day to honor dead relatives and ancestors. And Rocio said we could talk to the dead and that they would hear us. She looked straight into my eyes when she said, "You can ask for help to relieve the burdens of your sins."

Tio Rojelio took us to the plaza in his old pickup. The place was lit with lanterns and candles, vendors on every corner selling fruit, gum, *pan dulce, pescado frito.* Women stood on the cobblestone street corners patting tortillas onto a *comal,* stirring pots of steaming frijoles over open fires. We followed the procession to the outskirts of town up to the cemetery. Everyone wore black and skeletal death masks. Specters pranced down the road in front of men playing violins, guitars, trumpets. Old women in black dresses and shawls carried bouquets of marigolds, zinnias, black-eyed Susans, along with baskets of bread and sugar-candy skulls. At the head of the procession pall-bearers carried a weather-beaten rotting casket painted red and green. When we arrived at the gates of the cemetery, old man DEATH leapt out of the casket and began to dance a jig. People laughed and jeered as he chose his partners. The musicians strummed, *"El dia que me maten que sea de cinco balazos.* The day they kill me let it be from five bullet shots."

It was the dark of the moon and the night was black satin glittering with a million tiny tongues of light that swayed in a burning sea of incandescence. The women in black placed flowers and fruit and sugar skulls on the grave sites while musicians strummed their guitars. The black-and-white-clad jesters roamed through the crowds dancing and juggling. Young men swallowed fiery torches. Old men carried boxes of hard candy and chewing gum cast into tiny skulls, crosses, bones, and tiny plaster cadavers at work: a blacksmith, a nurse, a cowboy, a hairdresser. And everywhere were bright baskets of brilliant gold and burnt-orange marigolds. Mama bought us skeleton candies and toy ghosts made of ice cream sticks and crepe paper.

We found Great-aunt Rivera's grave and Mama put Daddy's picture next to it with a little bouquet, and Tio Rojelio shoved the white cross he had carved and painted into the ground. We got on our knees, and crossed ourselves, and prayed.

The priest came around later and blessed the cemetery with smoking incense and a chanted litany. Everyone was silent; only the wind stirred in the night, the dark night alight with candles, a sky of bright stars lighting up the rim of the earth. Bathed in the luminous darkness, I felt a shiver go up my spine. Looking into that vast glittering sea of life mingling with death on the border of twilight, I saw my father, pushing his way through the night toward me, arms flung out. And I heard his words echo, *Mi querida, preciosa, Carmelita.* For a flash of a second I felt his presence, a tingling hot surge inside me, opening my heart as a flame.

Early one morning we went with Tio to Mexico City for animal feed and medicine for his arthritis. Henry and I sat in the back of the truck. On the way there we stopped at the dump. The wind was blowing a horrible stench in our faces. I gagged. Henry held his nose pretending to vomit. We looked out to see a mountain of refuse and filth as big as a football stadium piled hundreds of feet high. On the top of it, ragged people were picking through garbage and junk with scarves over their mouths and noses. Lean-tos and cardboard shacks were scattered everywhere.

People were actually living here. My mind reeled, confused, unable to comprehend. I closed my eyes for a moment, dizzy and sick. I wanted to sink into the ground and disappear. Henry's eyes were wide, full of disbelief. I gathered my courage, willed myself to look. I could see where people had built shelters out of tattered dirty cardboard, old tires and corrugated tin. A woman in filthy clothes was cooking beans in a dirty pot as her baby crawled in the refuse.

Later I overheard Tio telling my mother that the people who lived off the garbage and trash heap spent all day collecting aluminum cans, bottles, rusty nails, old shoes, broken appliances to trade or sell. He said that some had been born there. Other families had lived on the garbage heap for generations. One man who had controlled it for years, El Jefe, had so many women that he might have over 120 children, and they all lived in the dump, scavengers and ragpickers. But the last of his wives had caught him seducing a young girl, and had plunged a butcher knife into his back. He had bled to death. So now there was a dispute in the garbage world as to who would take over the business. An older man whose family had been there for generations, or the eldest son of the Jefe? There was a war going on. Several people had been killed—knifed, shot down. Besides the violence, there was hepatitis and typhoid. Over the years factories and industry had dumped hazardous waste which caused a high incidence of cancer. Many children had died or were dying.

"Why do they stay?" I asked Tio.

"Porque, no saben que hacer. That's all they've ever known," he said.

Downtown we saw men standing at busy intersections spewing fire from their mouths. *"Tragafuego,"* Tio said.

"How do they do that?" I wanted to know.

"He holds gas in his mouth," my mother said, "and then lights it, spitting it out."

"Es peligroso. Very dangerous." Tio said. "Those boys don't live very long. They die young."

"But why do they do it?"

"See that money jar he has. He makes more than he would working a regular job, here in Mexico."

On our way to the doctor's, we drove past sprawling estates, walled-off fortresses with electrified wrought-iron fences and barred windows. *"Ay viven los ricos.* The homes of the rich," said Tio.

I stared, curious. I could not imagine what lay beyond those iron walls where no human life stirred. They looked completely empty, closed down, like prisons. And it occurred to me for the first time in my life that there must be an alien race cohabiting the earth. An inexplicable alien force.

On the way home we drove out past another sea of ramshackle hovels. A whole city of fetid, endless cardboard shacks. Over it all a rotten, odious stench of raw sewage and urine, a thick black suffocating smog, hung in the air like the promise of death. Not a quick and merciful dying, but a lingering hopeless purgatory.

I began to wonder if it was something I had done? Something bad, some sinful thought or deed like stealing or lying, or wishing someone dead? Was I being punished? Was that why my family had come here?

I had never really paid attention to the words *rich* and *poor, city* and *countryside.* Outside of Aunt Dede's, I had never really been anywhere besides Watsonville. Now as we drove through the capital past the wealthy estates, then through the squalor of the slums, I felt for the first time, felt in my bones, that there was evil in the world. And the thought occurred to me that I had died. And was in hell. I shuddered, closing my eyes, willing myself gone, to be home again. My father sitting in the kitchen, waiting for us. Did I love him? Did I hate him? I didn't know.

I was relieved to get back to the ranch, to the smell of the earth, the soil, the open fields. I walked out through the pasture, into the meadow, playing in the dirt, touching it, letting it sift through my palms, skipping through the wild flowers and the tall weeds, picking up rocks and twigs, crushing leaves in my fingers to breathe in the natural clean odor. I skipped around a big oak tree, brushed its bark with my fingertips, singing, "The farmer in the dell, the farmer in the dell, hi ho a dairy o, the farmer in the dell."

I sat under the tree, taking in its sweet odor, found an acorn and dropped it into my pocket. The sun had begun to set. I gazed out at the distant, somber, and majestic mountains, dusky rose, turning indigo, deep violet, overhead at the vast and luminous sky, at the open quiet fields, and for the first time realized it was *this*. This sacred *connection* to the ground and sky and mountain that had been wiped out, obliterated from that place, the city.

I stood transfixed, rocked in reverie, gazing at the mountain now engulfed in black shadows, as if trying to capture its essence, its vast mystical nature, as if it were a loving father I could hold in my mind's eye, in my childhood heart as a good luck charm, a wedge against sorrow and evil.

I headed for home, skipping toward the light at the ranch, my heart soaring. I felt as if I were flying. I was a very special child to be so close to God.

Suddenly, I became aware that it was almost dark. I began to run fast down the hill. As if something were chasing me, something out there in the night—the devil's tongue, bats, flying witches. I hit a rock, fell, tumbled head over heels, grinding my face into the hard-packed dirt. I began to cry and scream in terror.

I woke up in my bed. Rocio told me that Tio Rojelio had found me asleep outside. *"Fijate no mas, esta muchacha esta loca.* This little girl is crazy."

"Es cierto. It's true," my mother agreed.

Watching Ravens

Liza Prunuske

At first, Lou just imagined running down Ten Mile Road. She'd wear her new shoes, running shorts. "I'll be back in half an hour," she'd say.

But she wouldn't come back. She would keep running, through the state park, under the arching bays coated with dust, past Willow Creek and the rows of alder trees. She'd come to the highway, and there someone would pick her up. Maybe a ranch wife on her way to a waitress job in Bodega Bay. Maybe an old couple tooling down the coast in a creamy car. Maybe a man, just an ordinary man with thick hands and his arm resting on the open window.

Then she began to consider what to pack, how she could tuck an extra pair of shoes inside the edges of her one small suitcase, which sweater would make her feel bold. She kept the gas tank full. She bought some tapes, things that she would never let Ron see: Tammy Wynette, Prince, and even, hidden in the springs beneath the passenger seat, Elvis. Not a young, classic Elvis, but the fat old man in white bell-bottoms and jewels singing

"Suspicious Minds." Her errands took longer and longer as she drove slowly along back roads and felt his voice settling in her belly.

Ron, on the other hand, was becoming harder for her to hear. She tried to focus, to fit her attention to him as if they were two puzzle pieces that she should have been able to lock together. He complained about a plumbing contractor showing up late at the house he was working on that day. He wanted to know whether she thought he should fix the roof on the water tank before the rains started, or if they could wait another year. He didn't ask her when the ravens came that morning or if she wanted to touch the inside of his thigh, right there where his shorts ended.

She didn't feel like cooking anymore. And now that Thea and Rosie were both gone, she'd given up tallying nutrients. She could have lived on baked potatoes and new green grapes. She drank wine, not out of habit as she and Ron used to as soon as the kids were in bed, but submerged in the fragrance, the cool bite of it. Ron asked, "Is anything wrong?"

She had no answer.

In the morning, Lou is always turned away from me. I think she is really awake, but she keeps her eyes closed, even when I touch her. I feel like she has spent the night with another man.

I think that if I get up quietly and leave early for work, she will have more time alone. She always says she wants time alone. But it doesn't seem to help. Thea brushes it off, says it's just another one of Lou's stages, like the year she dragged us all to poetry readings. Rosie says she needs more fun. Go to Hawaii, she says, and for the first time in my life, I can see doing that. I would take Lou to Hawaii, find one of those big white beaches and we would just sit there, the two of us. I could spend a lot of time just watching Lou.

But I'm stuck right now. This is the worst time of year for me to leave the business. And I'm afraid Lou's job is in jeopardy. Jenny called me twice at work last week, wondering where the hell she was. It was 11:00 a.m. both times. Lou had meetings scheduled and she wasn't answering the phone at home. So what do I do? Kiss off my kids' tuition or try to help Lou?

I love my girls, but I've been looking forward to this year. This was supposed to be our time, mine and Lou's. But like I told Jenny, I don't know where she is.

Dear Rosie,

I am watching ravens as I write to you. There are seven now that come every day, late in the morning, to sit on the tops of the redwoods below the house. If I am very still and can keep Bill from barking at squirrels, I can hear them talking. They have a whole vocabulary, growly sounds and chirrups, and a slurred little whisper. Every time I listen, I think of the neighbor women coming to sit with my mother in their lawn chairs, their voices rough with cigarettes. It must have been spring, when the big kids were still in school. The women were oiled and shiny, drinking cokes or coffee from the percolator on the kitchen counter. I remember pillowcases and white shirts rising from the clothesline.

Of course, I haven't been getting much work done, staying home till the ravens fly away. I get to the office later and later, and then have to stay till seven or eight trying to catch up. I am tired all the time. Maybe you're right and I should stop drinking so much coffee. I should keep lists, give things to the Salvation Army.

Oh Rosie, I miss having you here. Tell me what you see out your windows. Tell me again.

Love,
Mom

After Mom's last letter came, I called home. This is getting too weird. Dad said she looks at him sometimes as if she doesn't know who he is. We talked her into flying here last Friday to spend the weekend with me. It's not quite Maui, but it was the best I could do on short notice.

The first night, she refused to take the bed and slept in my sleeping bag on the floor instead. I know it made her back hurt, but I promised Dad to save my lectures for important things.

Turns out, I didn't get a chance. I told Dad on Monday that I thought she'd gone feral. That's a new word from my wildlife class; I had to explain it.

Mom looks pretty much the same, her hair short and neat, the businesswoman's cut of the nineties, her regular jeans, same old stuff. But she doesn't say much. She's quiet and she watches. When we went out for pizza Saturday night with some of my friends, I think they forgot she was there. Usually she is the sparkly one, the center of attention. This time she sat in the corner hardly eating anything. I would have thought she was sick except that her eyes were so awake, like Bill's when he sees a gopher shaking the ground. And when she saw me looking at her, she smiled, not that dreamy one, but her real smile. Still, I was nervous.

After dinner and the movie, Mom and I walked out to the lake on the north end of campus. It was still pretty warm and there were a few loons left. Mom had never heard them calling. They migrate through Bodega Bay in the spring, but they only sing in their summer homes, here in the Midwest or in New England and Canada. Sometimes, on those rare nights when the eel-brains below me turn off their CD player before midnight, I can even hear them from my room.

We found a flat rock on the edge of the water to sit on. I whispered to her that we might get lucky. She gave me a quick, odd sort of look, then turned off the flashlight.

I haven't told this to Dad yet, but I think she made those loons come to us. After a while, she stood up and took off her sweatshirt and the sweater she wore under it. She still had on a little sleeveless shirt, something silky and whitish. Her arms looked fuller and more substantial than I remembered. She raised them high above her head, not impulsively but as if she had practiced this.

She stood, certain and silent, and they came. There was a half-moon and I could see their silhouettes, two of them, the long necks, that smooth sweep from head to bill. When they were about twenty feet away, one threw back its head and called the wildest, tenderest sound I've ever heard.

We waited until they swam away and then we just walked home, talking all the way about ordinary things, like what to get Thea for her birthday. I sat by the window watching shreds of cloud glide in and out of the circle of moonlight long after Mom had fallen asleep.

Lou saw the lake, small as a puddle, from the airplane window. How much more generous the world seems, she thought, when you can only see a part of it. Rosie had needed to return on the same shuttle bus that had taken them to the airport so that she wouldn't miss her botany class. Rosie. Lou had skipped at least one class a week when she had been in school. It had been a code of honor.

She could still feel her daughter's ardent hug, her cheek on Rosie's hair. "Call me when you get back," Rosie had said, worrying less, Lou suspected, of crashes than that her mother might never land. Lou had cupped her daughter's face in both hands and said nothing. Promises didn't come as easily to her as they used to.

A young man took the seat next to hers. She gave him the obligatory smile and turned back toward the window. She had hoped for solitude, some time between Rosie and California to be nowhere.

But she found herself glancing back at him. He had a wild mass of blonde dreadlocks falling almost down to his waist and he smelled familiar, something faint and clean, Ivory soap maybe. With some urgency, he pulled a battered hard-covered notebook out of his daypack, and then shoved the pack under the seat in front of him. Oh, no, she thought, surprised at her disappointment, he's going to stare out the window and write in a journal.

She was wrong. It was a sketchbook, and he immediately began to draw a little boy who was reading a comic book on the aisle seat kitty corner to theirs. He was amazingly quick and succeeded in capturing the boy's total absorption, evoking vulnerability with one soft stroke for the cheekbone, before the stewardess' reminder to buckle their seatbelts jerked the boy out of his comic.

The young man grinned at her. "I have to move fast," he said.

"That's beautiful," she said, still surprised. "You're good."

"Thanks," he answered and tucked the sketchbook back into his pack. "Are you going all the way to San Francisco?"

"Yes," she said. "And you?"

"Yeah. I've got an interview tomorrow at the Art Institute." He didn't seem a bit anxious. In fact, he reminded her of Rosie, supremely at home in the world. Not smug, just safe. He pulled out the airline magazine, tactfully withdrawing so that she could go back to looking out the window.

"Good luck," she said. He smiled at her, then turned to the article on surfing spots along the Big Island. She was profoundly grateful. Her eyes filled with tears. This is ridiculous, she thought. Maybe I'm starting menopause. If he were a little older, I would fall in love with him because he is reading a magazine.

She pulled out her own book, *A Life History of Jays, Crows and Titmice,* by Arthur Cleveland Bent. She had discovered it at the university bookstore while waiting for Rosie to finish her last class Friday. It was an old book, published in the 1920s, filled with strange anecdotes, most of them quoted from letters and journals so patiently and richly detailed that for a while she felt utterly satisfied. She read of ravens who had dropped rocks on mountain climbers' heads, of fledglings hanging by their beaks from linden branches, of a line of ravens taking turns sliding down a snowy hill on their bellies.

This time the young man was watching her.

"The stewardess wants to know if you want chicken or pasta for dinner," he said gently. Lou looked up to see the stewardess waiting and felt her cheeks flush.

"Uh, pasta would be fine." She was embarrassed, as if she had been caught in some private, intimate act. She took a deep breath. Oh, grow up, Lou. What on earth is happening? She closed her eyes and thought of Elvis. Did he ever feel like an adult? She tried to imagine him at a staff meeting or discussing funding strategies with one of her clients.

She could tell by the silence that her neighbor had stopped turning the magazine pages. If he looks worried, I will spill my ginger ale in his lap, she decided.

She opened her eyes. He did. She grabbed her glass, but he caught her eye and she merely raised it to her mouth. I almost did it, she thought, I almost spilled my drink on this guy on purpose and he knows it.

"I'm sorry. I hate it when people worry about me. It makes me feel responsible to them," she said, trying to sound reasonable and thinking that she really ought to ignore this and pretend that she had just jerked awake, maybe from some dream.

"You were crying," he said.

"I just want to feel what I feel without it being somebody's fault." She was tired and wanted to be home sitting with her dog in the yard. All the holes inside were empty again. Part of her couldn't believe that she was saying this to a total stranger.

"Okay," he said. "Okay."

Their lunches came. She ordered wine and offered to

buy him some too. He accepted. When it came, he raised his plastic glass to hers. "To jays and titmice, whatever they are," he said, and she laughed. They talked about San Francisco and she told him of all the places she loved there until the plane landed. When they reached the terminal, she hugged him hard and wished that she could follow him home, but he didn't ask.

The only good thing about airports at night is that it's easy to find a parking space. Even so, I didn't get here until after Lou's plane had landed. I needed to stop at Computerland in Serramonte and it took me longer than I thought. But I have what I need. We can take off for a couple of weeks now, and the business will manage.

I wonder how I can tell her. She will probably be angry, think I'm tricking her or being too protective. Or worse. Maybe she won't even care.

Sometimes I don't think I'm up to this. I think I'll just stick to building houses and let her go wherever she's going. But then I remember Lou crabby with her arms full of baby or Lou listening to me late some night, elbows on the table with her chin cupped in her hand.

She is waiting alone. Everybody else on her flight must have gone downstairs to claim their baggage. She has nothing except one small suitcase and her purse. All I can see is the back of her head and it scares me. She isn't even looking for me.

"Lou," I say, and she turns.

"Hi, Ron." She looks like she's been crying. "How are you?"

"I'm okay. Are you ready?" She nods and we walk to the car. Even friends or a brother and sister would hug each other. I want to smash her suitcase against the goddamn wall and scream, "Lou, what the hell is wrong?" But we keep on walking and when I open up the car door, she sinks in as if her legs can go no further.

"How was Rosie?" I ask after we clear the airport. That brings a little smile.

"She's Rosie. I think she's happy there." The night is unusually warm, and I roll down my window. We are on Nineteenth Avenue, passing San Francisco State where even this late at night, students wait for buses. I hear a girl calling to someone across the street.

"She took me to a lake to listen to loons," Lou offers. I search my memory for something about loons, anything to keep a conversation going, but there isn't much there. When I glance at her, she has turned both shoulders toward her window.

On the bridge I see the fog waiting just offshore, massive and cold. Parts of me are breaking, bursting inside. I think that if I say something, blood will come out of my mouth.

She wonders what he is doing. Ron pulls off the freeway at the Headlands exit and drives toward the overlook above the Golden Gate. He parks on the very edge. She could open her door and fly a thousand feet down.

"Lou," he says, "Look at me."

She drags her eyes to his. He is crying. "I don't know a thing about loons. Tell me something about them so I can talk to you."

What can she tell him? She has seen them glide out of the darkness, heard them, watched them go. Like

Rosie, like the young man on the plane, they are, they just are.

"I don't know about loons either." And then she feels a smile, unrepentant, even silly. "But I could tell you about ravens, Ron. I could tell you a lot about ravens."

Grace

I love her for throwing her baby on the bed,
my grandmother—in this country she was called Grace.
"Take him," she said to grandpa, as her anger rose
certain as bread kneaded in the bowl.
Six children, twenty-eight years old, that night
she would not cry, face like a stone.

The baking house was made of stone
picked from the fields or the creekbed.
It was old when she moved there. At night
the windows would be hollow, the grace
of women gathered, flour scraped from bowls,
had gone. She listened as dust rose

in a spear of setting light. Outside the roses
pressed into the window, brushing the stone
with soft, pink faces. She picked some for the glass bowl
in the center of the table, before the mending, before bed.
She was falling, but she could hope for grace,
the sweet, wild smell in her kitchen all night.

Maybe it would catch her, carry her away this one night,
return her to the kitchen before the sun rose,
before Frank came down grumbling, "Grace, Grace,
where is my coffee?" and Francis and Ralph, treasure stones
still tucked into their overall pockets, tumbled from bed.
She would punch the dough in the big silver bowl,

but she would be different. She would smile and the bowl
of roses on the table would glow, luminous as a snowy night.
Upstairs, in the dark bedroom, her side of the bed
would be cold. When the baby awoke, skin rose-
blushed and chuckling, he would not cry, not stone
her morning hope down with his colicky whine, but grace

this day and this night with the astonishing grace
of contentment and there would be four fresh loaves and a bowl
of pink roses, too, gathered at dusk from an old stone
house. But as she darned, Baby screamed in the night
and with yarn and worn socks spilling from her lap, she rose
quick as always, and climbed the stairs to the cradle by her bed.

There Frank slept. Babies were Grace's and the night
was his. Burning in their bowl of stones and water, the roses
cursed the bread, tore free her tongue and shattered petals on her bed.

Beginning

Elizabeth Herron

To begin with, there were no endings, and so we walked around and around, unable to stop our feet from the changing landscape. Till at last, exhausted and hungry, we stopped to gather berries and the edible mosses that grew along the banks of the river. The four-footed creatures lapped the silky water and then dozed, leaning vague into each other since the gully sloped sharply, throwing them off balance. In this way they grew calm, calmer, and still more calm till the least they could do was dream the dreams of drowsing horses on hot summer days under cottonwoods, or the dreams of deer at midday cupped in meadow grass. Some sank deeper into the dreams of winter marmots, whose blood slowed to a near stop, and in whose quiet brains the long rhythms of the earth were perfectly echoed.

Only we remained alert, waiting for what we were certain we would momentarily recall. We watched the easy habitual glide of trout under the ledge of rock, below where in the clear water we could see each pebble. We witnessed each soft shushing of the willows in the wind. We waited and kept watch while the others slept, and after a time, our watching became a prayer, for what is prayer but the rising of joy in our bodies, the fervent heat of happiness we feel when our watching ceases to be separate from the watched, and in our observation we discover the perfect stillness of the thundering rush of utter miracle that this, this, this, is.

Oh, I know there are prayers from despair and desperation but these prayers, our prayers then, were from the place where separation falls away and here now becomes the heart, the center, the source itself, where delight overcomes terror, and understanding is a flood of light that pours forth from each discreet and incandescent moment, each blade of grass, each hair on the coat of the beast, each slight shift in the angle of even shadow.

Poised there we waited, till the waiting too was lost, and even memory was merely part of present. How long we remained thus I cannot say, perhaps hours, perhaps generations, for the knowledge of that place resides in everyone. And who is to say where it began, since there were no endings? And who is to say you were not there, for surely you remember now, don't you? And who is to say that this is not the very place? Listen, don't you hear it—the rush of stillness? And look, see the light flooding forth from those beside you? Look at your hands. See how they shine? See how luminous even your clothes have become, holding your light? See how that light is held, even in shadow?

Place

When we arrived we saw as if only the great light of the place and how each narrow moment held the whole openness of time so once again we could imagine ourselves into it. We saw the tiny flowered forget-me-nots scattered like blue stars through the woods under the shelter of the heavy oaks, and further, on the sloping banks of the river, how thick the willows grew, how lush with the layers of song of the nesting sparrows.

All spring the overcast promised an end to the long drought that had driven us from the old place, and rain spattered and patted the earth and all upon it lightly more than once a quarter moon those first four moons of our coming.

As the grasses grew tall and small seeds ripened at their tips (rattle grass, and silk grass, quail grass and red grass), we came together there—all of the many from the great and small tribes of the earth. From all directions we came, some families thin with only one or two cousins, some fat with uncles and aunts. Even solitary couples came, and a few lone travelers. But among them all, there were few—a mere handful of elders, and of infants we counted only three, for the winter had been cold, the game sparse and cunning, and the journey perilous.

Whenever another arrived, we celebrated, for we felt blessed to find each other after the generations of separateness, and our hearts were glad to know we had not lost the lore and stories of our beginning, which were carried in the tales of the old ones, and would (we were certain now) be told in ages to come, for already some of the women grew large with new life, and there was plenty to eat, and we dared hope again for the cries of birth, and for children's laughter brightly flying through the village.

There was much to occupy us in this new place where the earth was familiar and yet strange. The plants needed for healing had to be gathered and dried, and even then we could not be certain, and so some were boiled undried to test their powers. And we must study the habits of the local game, follow the trails of the four-footed ones, watch the streams for our water friends, and prepare for the many ceremonies these new creatures would require, for the chants and songs of the old place must be aligned with the new if we were to honor this only half-familiar world.

And there was sadness, too, for what was gone forever but lived on in our hearts, and for the bones of those who had crossed the great darkness, for we could not carry their bones when we came, and we had to leave them where they lay, back in the old land, along with our treasured places—each her own, as mine had been the rock on the river under the overhanging alders, and it would be a long time before I stopped weeping for that rock and those alders and the river of then, though I took comfort in the sweet water and kind rocks and trees of the place, where we now spread our blankets.

To Cathy,
thanks for reading —
Miriam Silver

The Leaves, They Keep Falling

Miriam Silver

Hearing my new guy called by the name of the old one I am trying to forget ever existed is not my idea of a great way to start the morning.

But Dorrie, my neighbor, likes to call Nick, Robert. I hate it, but Nick won't correct her. It is one of the nicer things about Nick, the meaner things about me and the more annoying things about Dorrie.

"Hi, Robert," Dorrie says to Nick just about every morning while she waits for her bus. "Hi, Robert."

Dorrie is a hulk of a woman, nearly six feet tall and big-boned. Her short brown hair is usually clean but always messy, like a little tomgirl's. Dorrie is thirty-five.

The day I move into my first house, Dorrie stands outside welcoming me to the neighborhood.

"Hey, you work for the newspaper, right? Are you the new neighbor?"

"Right," I say, wondering if living in the town where I work is such a good idea after all.

"Well, we didn't get our newspaper this morning. The paperboy hardly ever gets it here."

"But I'm just a reporter. We don't handle delivery," I say.

But she says the same thing again. Either she doesn't hear me or she is just ignoring me.

"We didn't get our newspaper. Can you get us one?"

No point in arguing while dragging in heavy boxes. "Okay, I'll see what I can do."

I hate that association with the newspaper. People always seem to be more interested in sports, the weather, their horoscopes and getting the paper thrown on their front porch. News is not a priority.

"Hey, are you the new neighbor?" Dorrie keeps repeating herself. I am getting annoyed. "Can I have some figs? Mrs. Olstrom gave me figs before she left."

I bought the house from Mrs. Olstrom's estate. Mrs. Olstrom died alone. Neighbors say she once had beautiful roses. But when she could no longer take care of them, she had them torn out, somehow thinking that an untended garden would signal to robbers that an old, helpless woman lived inside. All that's left is a hugely overgrown fig tree, the crowning glory of the backyard of an otherwise godforsaken little cottage I am going to try and make home.

"Can I have some figs? I always got figs from Mrs. Olstrom," says Dorrie.

"Yes, of course. When the figs are ripe, you can help yourself."

Besides being friendly and big and a pest, Dorrie, I finally figure out, is developmentally disabled, or, as we used to say when I was a kid, retarded. She lives with her elderly parents, her dog Madeline, goes to a workshop three days a week, and stocks grocery shelves the other two days.

To Dorrie, Nick is Robert because the first day I move in, she meets Robert. Robert and I split up after ten years, and vow to stay friends forever. We manage to hold to that childlike promise for a few months, and that is why Robert is helping me move into my new house. Nick is there, too. We are such a cozy group, all three of us friends. So maybe Dorrie gets a little confused. Who wouldn't?

But as relationships go, soon there is less of Robert in the neighborhood and more of Nick. Robert puts in new locks on the door for me. Nick later builds the deck. Soon Nick is walking my dog and picking up the morning newspaper. And Robert stops visiting. Often, I get confused.

But to Dorrie it is all the same. Robert is the name of the guy who hangs around my house. Even though it really is Nick.

"Hi, Robert," says Dorrie. "I am going to work now."

The greeting jolts me. For a minute I think, My God! Robert is back. No, no. That's just Dorrie.

When the newspaper does arrive successfully on Dorrie's front porch, I discover her interest goes beyond delivery. She is an avid reader and seems to know more about what is in the news than most of my editors.

Her favorite stories are crime stories. And often she tells me the stories before they even get in the paper.

"Rachel, come on outside," Dorrie calls to me. "That boy is getting arrested."

Standing right at my front window is Dorrie, a Gulliver of a person peering inside. I am startled.

"C'mon," she says. "It's a drug bust."

I follow her outside. Sure enough, most of my neighbors are standing on their front lawns, like they do on the Fourth of July to watch the fireworks, and looking at the rundown duplex across the street. Two policemen are handcuffing our neighbor whose name we don't know, while a third walks around with a German shepherd.

"A drug bust," Dorrie says. "See?"

She is right. Next day, page four, under crime briefs: "Speed lab bust at 738 Oak Place."

Not all of Dorrie's tips are solid. It is on another morning that Dorrie announces a man has gotten shot at the 7-11 store.

"Right in the head. He's dead."

"No, Dorrie, really? When did it happen? Did he have an accomplice? What kind of gun?" I like interviewing Dorrie. She is certainly more forthcoming, if not as reliable as the people I usually deal with.

"Dead. In the head."

As soon as I go to work I call the cops and ask about the shooting.

"Nothing today, Rachel. Pretty quiet. A shoplifting at the 7-11, that's all."

Besides an interest in the news and mixing up my men, Dorrie and I have something else in common. Dogs. She has one and I have one. Mine is a mutt named Abigail. Hers is a mutt named Maddy, short for Madeline, a small, patchwork black and white dog with a piercing bark that gets worse when you talk to her. Dorrie's voice is as thick and strong as Maddy's is shrieking.

In a different life, Dorrie might have been a tenor or

a cattle caller.

Loud and clear across the yards, I hear Dorrie talking to Maddy. Usually I am working, or some friends are over, and Dorrie's voice cuts sharply into our conversation.

"Maddy. Hi. I'm home. Maddy, Maddy, where's my little Maddy?" Maddy yaps. Dorrie bellows. The voice of an older woman talking baby talk to her best friend, a ratty looking mongrel.

Not so much different from me, though. Often, there I am, baby-talking to my little brown and white beagle mutt. "Abby, baby. Give Mom a kiss." Abby will bark and bark while I laugh and yell. Nick says I sound just like Dorrie.

In the fall Dorrie rakes the leaves from the walnut tree in her front yard. I say, "Hi," and ask her what she is doing.

"The leaves. They keep falling," she says.

"Yeah," I say, "All that work every year, huh."

"I raked them yesterday. They keep falling. The leaves."

I stop and look at her. It sounds silly at first. Of course leaves fall. But then I think again. Dorrie is right. She sees it much more clearly than most of us, who never really get it when it comes to raking leaves.

"The leaves. They keep falling." She just can't understand why they keep falling. Well, who does?

Next morning and every morning until the winter rains wash off all the leaves, Dorrie is raking, saying the exact same thing as if it were the first time.

"The leaves. They keep falling."

I remember when I was little, a retarded kid lived on

our street. His name was Stevie, Stevie Janner. Stevie had parents much older than the rest of ours. He was tall and geeky. His Madras shirts were buttoned all the way up and he only came home to visit once in a while. Maybe it was because of the way we treated him.

"Hey, retardo. Hey, Stevie-weevie. Come climb a tree with us, Stevie."

We'd throw things at him and taunt him until his mother came out. Mrs. Janner was a small woman, and she'd reach up to his shoulders, put her arms around him, and quietly walk him inside. She always looked so tired and so old. Then he'd go back to his place, wherever that was, and we'd find something else bad to do, like soap a neighbor's house with curse words. I felt sorry for Stevie. He used to get so mad at us. But still, I teased him.

That's how we treated kids like Stevie. Stevie was probably one of the lucky ones. He only saw us once in a while. The ones who went to our school, the ones in the "special" classes, they got it a lot worse. They'd walk together through the hallways, bunched up like a caterpillar, and we'd hiss at them. They sat apart at lunch, with their teacher hovering at the head of their table. They'd laugh and talk and seem oblivious of us until we attacked. "There goes the circus. Look at the animals in the circus." We'd hoot like owls and scream like monkeys until the teacher threatened to send us to the principal's office.

It is a warm evening in early summer. The sun is still high and, with all the windows open, I can hear Dorrie yelling, all charged up about something. I am trying to work and cannot block out her voice.

Dorrie is standing in front of her tree, yelling at some kids down the street. Two boys, about eleven, are waving tree branches.

"We can take what we want. Want to come get us?" they shout.

"You can't take that off our tree. You can't do that. You can't take that off our tree," says Dorrie. The boys hide behind a fence and then pop out.

"You're ugly. We'll take as many walnuts as we want." And one of the boys starts rolling the nuts down the street.

Dorrie picks up her gardening shears and runs toward the boys.

"The police will arrest you. You can't take that off our tree." She thumps after them.

Oh, I don't want to get involved. I need to work. But someone has to do something. Where are Dorrie's parents? Surely they can hear this. I look at her house, curtains closed, as always. Her parents are older, much older. Her father uses a walker and her mother always looks tired. Nobody comes out. Her parents probably have fought these battles before.

I pull on some shoes and run outside. Damn these bratty boys. Why can't they leave her alone?

"Dorrie, come on home, now. Don't worry about them." She is so much bigger than I am. I touch her fleshy arm. I try to pull her. She resists.

"They took a branch. They took the walnuts. They can't take that off our tree."

The boys are laughing hysterically. One juggles walnuts, flashing them in Dorrie's eyes.

"Dorrie, come home now. Forget them. They're dumb. C'mon. Come back," I say.

She looks at me and her weight eases, toward me,

moving in my direction. She comes with me. I keep a firm hand on her back, prodding her home, away from the boys.

"You know Samuel in the hospital?" she says.

I stop for a second and look at her. Why is she talking about Samuel now? Samuel is an old man who lives alone in the one-bedroom blue house at the corner.

"That old man. Today. An ambulance came and got him. His heart. Samuel in the hospital. Today."

That quickly Dorrie changes topics. As if nothing else just occurred. She is in the present again. That she can be that way is a gift, I think. It is something I wish I could do.

Winter has come now. We had one rain. Nick and I are digging holes for tulip bulbs and I notice Dorrie standing under her walnut tree. She is unusually still and quiet. She looks up into the thinning branches.

"Whatcha' doing, Dorrie?" I ask.

"Waiting. For the leaves," Dorrie says. "They keep falling."

The Hitchhikers

Doris B. Murphy

When we were twelve, my best friend Margie and I cut each other's wrists and combined our blood. We believed this made us sisters for life. Since the first grade, she and I had managed not to be separated for any appreciable length of time. We planned to marry brothers someday and live in adjoining houses. When my parents moved to Phoenix from Portland for a three-year stay, I remained in Portland, living first with Margie's parents and then attending a boarding school.

We were eighteen and it was early summer. Soon it would be time for us to go to college. We had decided we would like to attend the University of Arizona where romance was sure to flourish. This was not on our parents' agenda. Margie's mother and father believed she should attend the University of Oregon. Mine believed the University of Arizona, one hundred miles from Phoenix, would be a suitable choice for me. Both sets of parents were wary of our attending the same school away from parental supervision. We had a reputation for getting into trouble when together too long.

My father had sent me train fare with instructions to return to Phoenix for the remainder of the summer. Margie's parents said she must remain at home. What should we do? The idea of just walking away took root. The more we played with this fantasy of leading a nomadic existence, the more "just hiking down the highways and byways of life," as we phrased it, appealed to us. One warm evening as we sat on the river bank near her home, we looked at each other and voiced the same thought: "Let's hitchhike to Arizona."

We whispered in the night under the bedclothes, we giggled and we argued about details, we made elaborate plans, we imagined impossibly exciting scenarios, we were pleasantly apprehensive and also excited by the inherent dangers ahead. Finally at dawn one July morning we donned our jodhpurs and riding boots so that we would look respectable, as if out for a canter, and slipped quietly from Margie's parents' home. Real honest adventure was our goal.

The highway to California was just off the road from Margie's country home, so that we were soon on our way to California via Salem, Eugene, Medford and points south. When we reached Medford shortly after noon, having received lifts by a series of helpful drivers, we wired our parents telling them of our plans but giving no clue regarding our route or any way in which they could reach us. It was the Fourth of July. We sat on a rock wall in front of a house located on Main Street. We watched the Independence Day Parade along with others from the small town, saluted the flag as it passed by, and clapped with the rest of the audience. We felt very smug at being accepted as members of this small farm community, aware that we were playing our part well. After the parade, we strolled to the edge of town where we were picked up by a local couple on their way to Klamath Falls. We casually discussed the merits of the various parade floats with the unsuspecting couple.

We had made an agreement to accept rides only with women or couples, never with only men in a car. In the early evenings we would stroll into a nice hotel with a fanciful story of losing our horses. We appeared to be so eminently respectable, that no one seemed to doubt or question us. We would spend the night in a pleasant hotel, have a shower, and strike forth the next morning, delighted with ourselves and our adventure. We had no luggage and kept our small cache of money, lipsticks, combs, and compacts in makeshift bags which had begun life as patch pockets on my raincoat. These we had attached to the belts of our riding pants.

We had rides on hay trucks, rides in new model sedans, rides in pickups. We told one outrageous story after another to our interested drivers. No one appeared to suspect that we were two eighteen-year-old girls hitchhiking to Arizona. This was 1930, not long after the Crash, and the beginning of the Great Depression. We were only vaguely aware of the disaster which had changed so many lives. When one older couple mentioned that they were thinking of moving to southern California or Arizona where there might be better employment opportunities, we murmured a sympathetic response, but truly had little understanding of their problem. Life for us was of the moment, and anything so remote as financial disaster was beyond either our understanding or our interest.

We traveled without a road map, and had only a vague idea of the fastest route south. A preplanned itinerary was of no interest to us. After all, we had all summer. Our small amount of cash would not last indefinitely, but we chose not to think about it. One sweltering hot afternoon we were sauntering down a road in northern California, not sure exactly where we were, when two friendly boys about our age offered us a ride.

"Do you girls live in Santa Rosa?" one of them asked.

"Oh no, we are visiting friends the other side of Santa Rosa and went for a horseback ride with horses rented from a stable up the way."

"Where?"

"Oh, just over there," we replied, waving vaguely in the direction from where we had come.

One of the boys said, "We were on our way to go swimming in the Russian River. Would you like to come along with us?"

We had no idea where the river was, but it was a very hot day. These boys seemed nice, much like those we knew at home. "We have no bathing suits," I said.

The most attractive of the boys answered grandly, "Oh, my sister and her friend have plenty of bathing suits. We'll drive by my house and get them."

His house was a big rambling affair with enormous shade trees. He introduced us to his mother, who looked puzzled when, in response to her question, we gave a fictitious identity for the friends we were supposedly visiting. But we seemed like such nice girls! How could she doubt us? She brought us lemonade and supplied us with bathing suits. Mine did not fit very well over my tall skinny frame, and Margie's fit too tightly over her more rounded body, but we were happy with this momentary turn of events.

We went swimming in the river, which seemed dirty to us, accustomed to the clean Willamette flowing past Margie's home where we had swum since childhood. We did not voice this comparison because we were so appreciative of the cool water and the boys were so pleasant and appeared to be so delighted with us. Around dusk they reluctantly left us on the Redwood Highway. We said we would prefer to walk to our friends' home. Down the highway a bit we were offered a ride by a friendly couple who drove us to Oakland, where we said we had relatives. We were disappointed to arrive in Oakland, having expected to land in glamorous San Francisco.

But we had told the truth about relatives. My recently married older brother Raeford lived in Oakland. I had no intention of calling him. He had married a very proper girl from a good family in Portland. They would not, could not, should not, be part of our fine adventure.

I remembered that my mother had a lifelong friend who lived in Oakland. I had always called her "Auntie Irene" at her request. I had never fully understood this friendship between Mrs. Vandecarr and my very conventional mother. Auntie Irene was a wealthy widow lady with jet black hair and a voluptuous figure. I thought her to be very sophisticated and "modern." She and her son, Rene, often visited us in Portland bearing expensive house gifts. Once, when I was about fifteen, she had brought me a shiny blue leather handbag with my initials engraved in gold. I treasured this gift for years. Something about her had always seemed to me to be slightly mysterious and perhaps even wild. "Wild" expressed it all when I was eighteen. She probably smoked cigarettes and even drank a cocktail when she was home alone. Such were my fantasies about this lady.

So I called Auntie Irene. "Oh, my dear, it is nearly midnight. Come to my apartment. Take a taxi. I will pay for it. Why are you out alone at nearly midnight? Where is your dear mother? Have you called Raeford?"

I had never known anyone who lived alone in an apartment. We were ushered into a room filled with French antiques, heavy dark furniture, pillows on chairs, and couches on the floor. It seemed a mysterious and slightly wicked room. Her son, Rene, who had recently finished medical school and whom I had thought the most handsome boy-man alive when he was around twenty-one or twenty-two and I was about ten, was now a dashing thirty. She called him for advice. He told her to call my brother Raeford.

Both men arrived in short order. Rene looked curiously and amusedly at the two bedraggled girls who had arrived so unexpectedly out of the night. Raeford looked embarrassed by our very existence, disgusted with what he saw as a spectacle that somehow demeaned him. They all conferred, ignoring any remarks from us. What a disappointment Auntie Irene had turned out to be. Why couldn't she just put us up for the night and let us be on our way in the morning?

"Oh, but what would your dear mother say? I cannot take that responsibility."

They debated whether or not to call our parents. Rene smiled engagingly, and said, "Don't blow the whistle on them, Mother. Why don't you just take them home with you, Rae?"

Mrs. Vandecarr wanted to call our parents. This would somehow teach everyone a lesson. A lesson about what? I failed to see the problem. Somehow both Margie's and my parents were to blame for our transgressions. Rae finally and reluctantly said he would take us home with him, but he would first have to call his wife, Ruth, to get her approval. Would his marriage be in jeopardy if he didn't get her permission?

That night we washed our underwear and dirty denim riding shirts in my sister-in-law's immaculate newlywed's bathroom, all blue and perfumery. Things were strained the next morning at breakfast.

To break the tension I said, "I wonder what our shirts thought, being washed?"

Silence, and then, "I wonder what my expensive hand soap thought being used to wash dirty shirts," Ruth replied.

We were clearly unwelcome. They promised not to call our parents and allowed us to set forth again without offering so much as an extra dollar or a word of affection. So much for relatives. Let us praise the kindness of strangers.

That evening we arrived in Pasadena, at a respectable hour, feeling refreshed from our perfumed baths and clean clothes. We registered at one of the better hotels, splurged on dinner from our rapidly diminishing funds, and sat on the rooftop in the moonless night, admiring the brilliance and the nearness of the southern California stars.

It took us two days to cross the Mojave Desert and

parts of Death Valley. Our last ride of the second day was in the back of a pickup truck driven by two sun-tanned ranchers. Our faces were burned red and felt raw when, totally exhausted by the sun and desert wind, we reached Hicksville, California, a small border town about 100 miles northwest of Yuma, Arizona. It was dusk and night was fast approaching. Hicksville, appropriately named, was a wide spot in the road. We saw only one possible place for us to spend the night, a ramshackle structure which appeared to be neither safe nor private. There was a sinister aura about the building, although we were hard-put to define it, or perhaps we were overly tired and our imaginations had taken over. The inhabitants of the town, who slouched in and out of a noisy bar, had an unsavory look about them. We saw few women and those whom we might have approached ignored our presence. We were conspicuous and out of place. After long consultation over a hamburger in a dreary coffee shop, we decided to abandon our plan of never traveling after dark.

We faced 100 miles of desert between us and Yuma, Arizona. We started down the long black highway, refusing rides from the first several cars, cowboys and ranch hands out for a lark. Everyone seemed drunk. As night began to fall we finally admitted that we were frightened. Then a large black sedan slowed and two well-dressed middle-aged men offered us a ride. As we entered the car we were overwhelmed with the stench of stale whiskey.

We knew immediately that we had not chosen well. We sat in the back seat and looked at each other with apprehension. We had driven only a few miles when the car slowed to a stop. One of the men got out and asked us to disembark.

"Is there car trouble?" I asked, knowing full well there was none.

He replied, pleasantly enough, "No trouble, we thought it would be more friendly if one of you girls rode up front with Frank and I rode in back with the other one."

We hesitated; we knew each other's mind. For all of our swaggering and bravado we were aware that we were in trouble. While the three of us stood awkwardly on the highway shoulder, a car driving back toward Hicksville approached. Margie and I ran to the middle of the highway screaming, "Stop! Stop!" Our benefactors jumped into their car and sped away. The passing motorist did not stop. It was very dark. There was no moon. We were alone on the highway with miles and miles of our romanticized, no longer friendly, desert reaching into infinity.

Margie's imagination often ran to the dramatic. "If we walk into the desert, we could be bitten by a rattlesnake. We don't dare sleep here; there are Gila monsters and they might attack us."

I said, "What should we do, go back to Hicksville or start walking to Yuma?" Neither plan was attractive. Several cars passed and we crouched out of sight in the sagebrush, fearful of whoever might stop. Perhaps those dreadful men would return. The night seemed to darken further as we became more frightened and more desperate.

Eventually a large commercial truck stopped, with a lone truck driver who spoke with concern. "What are you girls doing out here at night?"

We hopped into the cab and told him the true story

of our predicament. He drove us back to Hicksville, wished us good night and good luck and went on his way. He had a load to deliver in the next town. It was now after midnight. The small ugly town was asleep. An unshaven night clerk looked at us without interest. He gave us a key to a dingy room. A screened door opened onto a long porch. The key was symbolic only. Other rooms also opened onto the porch. We could hear muffled voices as well as the guttural sounds of sleeping men who had drunk too much. We lay fully dressed on the iron bed with the straw mattress, but did not sleep. At one point, someone rattled our screen door and a voice muttered an obscenity. We lay very quiet, hardly breathing; then the voice moved away and into the night. In our innocence we thought it was just a strange and weird place. But it was, of course, a brothel.

Eternities later, there was an unattractive dawn. We dashed tepid water on our faces and fled into the desert to meet the unrelenting sun. The highway looked less threatening in the daylight. We still had to cross it to get to Yuma, and then make it from Yuma to Phoenix. This was the last leg of our trip; we had been traveling for eight days. By now our adventure had lost much of its glamour and we could think only of a long luxurious bath, clean clothes and, as I said to Margie, "A cherry coke with lots of chipped ice." It was midsummer and the desert was much hotter than we had remembered it to be.

A middle-aged couple drove us to Yuma and went on their way after dropping us, at our request, at the "best hotel in town." Our only thought was to get to Phoenix without further mishap. We freshened up in the hotel's public restroom, then had breakfast in the coffee shop.

We planned our strategy. This time we must play it safe. We appealed to the hotel manager. I gave my father's name for identification, remembering that he had told me several years earlier that if I were ever in trouble I must tell someone who my father was.

I had not understood what he meant at the time. Now I did. We asked the manager if he knew if any of his hotel guests were driving to Phoenix that day. If so, would he ask them, for us, for a ride? He was stiff and remote and suspicious. He looked us over carefully. He went away and we continued to sit in the booth drinking coffee. Later an older couple walked by, gave us the once-over, and walked on. We were discouraged. Would we have to telephone home and admit we couldn't do this on our own? Would our great adventure end so mundanely with a phone call, "Please, Daddy, come and get us"? How humiliating.

Finally two respectable-looking men in suits and ties sauntered past, walked away, returned and spoke to us. "Which one of you is Luther Bailey's daughter?"

"I am."

The men looked skeptical, but they drove us to Phoenix, talking quietly to each other. We felt snubbed as we sat silently in the back seat, finally humbled and somewhat chastened, the bravado gone. In Phoenix the men deposited us at a bus stop at our request. We walked up to my parents' home with trepidation but also with a sense of triumph. We had made it! My nine-year-old brother Jack was hanging out on the patio.

When he spotted us he said gleefully, "Oh boy, are the folks mad at you! Oh boy, are you two going to get it!"

My mother was out. We bathed luxuriously, found the clothes we had mailed home and adorned ourselves in summer dresses. We felt charming. And then my parents roared in, my mother looking concerned, my father looking enraged.

"How could you do this to us? How could you humiliate us so?"

The men who had driven us to Phoenix from Yuma were business acquaintances of my father and had gone directly to his office after depositing us at the bus stop.

After the explanations and after the story of our more recent adventure, my parents expressed relief at our safe arrival. But we were not forgiven.

During the remainder of the summer we swam at the country club pool and rode horseback down shaded paths. When it became known that we planned to attend the University of Arizona in Tucson, we were "rushed" by some of the Phoenix sorority girls. We dated the local boys; one double date was Barry Goldwater, Jr., the son of the owner of the Goldwater Department Store. That he would later become the Republican candidate for president and belligerent conservative politician was certainly not obvious. To us he was only a rather nice-looking and courteous man-about-town, not especially interesting. We were so unimpressed with him that later we could not remember whether it was Margie or I whose date he had been.

We spoke to none of our new friends about the hitchhiking episode. Instead of a great adventure, my parents and Margie's let us know that this was our secret disgrace, not to be discussed with anyone. For years we behaved as if it had never happened.

The Wish Fulfilled

Mimi Luebbermann

I always wished to live in the country on a farm, surrounded with chickens, cats, dogs, trees, fresh air, and space. When I first moved into my house in Oakland, I swore I would only live there for ten years. Twenty-three years later I was still mired. Not only did I live there, but I had two children in school, an attic stuffed with broken furniture and baby clothes, a basement filled with unfinished projects, and a workshed full of tools, lawn chairs, my ex's art work, and enough bicycle parts to put a fifth-grade class on wheels. Of course, there was also my office and a garden of plants blooming in containers. I was rooted to that place.

The dream of moving to the country seemed absurd. Yet I had been practicing that move for twenty-three years, even keeping chickens. Chickens in Oakland? Once I even got an obscene phone call from a neighbor because he couldn't stand the sound of cackling when chickens laid their eggs. I vowed someday to have roosters. Vegetables took up a portion of the yard edged by towering apple trees, and, in the summer, the apples provided such a harvest of organic fruit that the kids made money selling them to local restaurants. I worked in the converted garage, an efficient office with huge glass doors that looked out on the garden and a delft-blue rug that stayed almost clean because the boys rarely came in, usually just standing at the door to ask for a snack.

I told myself that I didn't really need to move to the country, truly I didn't want to, this whim was just a midlife crisis reversion to my childhood farm life, which precipitously ended with the family move to Florida when I was seven. I was perfectly happy in my mature urban sophisticated life, in my house, in Oakland. Both the house and garden had grown into just the right mix of casual and formal, my friends were within walking distance, San Francisco was the perfect travel range, and, to top it off, the neighborhood had become coffee bar chic. Why should I move?

I couldn't help it. I ground my teeth every time I heard the neighbor's toilet flush, I turned the radio up loud so I couldn't hear another neighbor's phone, his dog bark. Despite all my reasoning to stay put, something felt as if it were stuck in my throat. A force in between my shoulder blades seemed to push me along, like a mother firmly guiding her recalcitrant child.

I began to tuck notes to myself on the side of the computer screen—affirmations, childish chitter-chatter, a kind of absurd conversation with myself about how it was going to be in the country, and how it would be okay if a fifty-year-old woman moved alone to the country, without country knowledge, without children, without friends. My mother's voice cheerily answered me, "Don't worry, dear, you can always make new friends." The silent conversations echoed like a sound loop in my brain.

As if under alien control, I painted the outside of the house and invited an old friend to be my realtor. I began to clean out the attic and go for drives in the country, looking longingly at the farms next to the road. With a sense of the unreal, I continued to write notes to myself on the computer, sometimes bursting into tears when I reread them. My city house was in itself a dream come true, representing family, love, kinship, neighborhood. I had moved in with a child and a husband, and soon had two children and then no husband.

Selling the house was admitting that a part of my life was over. No more husband, no more kids, no more strolling up and down our street so familiar I could almost walk it blindfolded. Underneath the flowering plum trees, I had walked behind strollers, chatted up the neighbors, followed children on their first push bikes, then "big wheels," then bicycles, and then of course they were off on their own in cars. How could all the time go so quickly? One minute children were in diapers, the next they were into their own world.

I had to ask myself what it would mean to leave the house, the memories, the sound of the wind in the winter when it keened around the bathroom windows. I was selling the family home, where my children had been raised—the doorway marked with their heights, their rooms and adjoining sunny porches where they built Lego cars, ran the little wooden train, and set up the slot car racing track. What about the big wide stairway they slid down on pillows, whooping with joy when they crashed into the comforter-padded landing? What future was I building for myself, what past was I destroying for my children? I had no answers, only the compelling need to move on.

I had to throw out and pack up, sort old dreams, save rags of past memories, give away bits and pieces of myself to friends and neighbors as tokens of our years next to each other, linked by sidewalk parties, adolescent disasters, the clanging ambulances that came in the night. I kept digging out, sifting, saving, discarding, from floor to floor, and then the attic suddenly was clean and empty as it had been when I first walked up the stairs and found the hidey-hole under the stairs we called "the safe." Empty, the closets, empty, the rooms, empty, echoing, hollow, and the house no more mine. Neutral, stripped, impersonal, ready to absorb the next owner's dreams.

Gaining one dream means leaving another, for as you cross one threshold into new, you leave old. "For every forward motion there is a corresponding backward motion." I suppose that is what I am doing, pushing, pummeling, cajoling, driving, launching, bolstering, and pitching myself out of the old and into the new. So one door has shut, and another has opened, and my dream has come true. I wished for it.

The Brush

J. J. Wilson

Somehow, in the confusion of traveling, my one good hairbrush had disappeared, and thus early that first day in Istanbul, I ventured out into the veiled streets in search of a replacement. Feeling that kind of loneliness that comes to me in large cities, I wandered through the exotic markets with their spices, copperware, leather, and rugs, finding finally a more everyday kind of shop. In the cluttered store-window display, my eyes focused on something that looked as if it might be a hairbrush. I also became aware of a young woman peering out at me from inside the store. Our eyes met. I mimed the universal gesture of brushing hair and pointed to the object in question. She nodded vigorously and so I entered the shop ready to count out the unfamiliar Turkish money and be quickly on my way with my much-needed purchase.

Perhaps she found my coiffure in need of her attentions, or was it just a slow morning? Whatever the reason, she seemed to feel my arrival was a special occasion; having a travel-worn tourist with tangled hair under her hands, she knew just what to do. Before I realized what was happening, she had me seated on a low stool and was slowly, tentatively, and then with ever more firmness, using my new brush as if to demonstrate its excellence, as well as her willingness to serve my need. I do not know how long she took with her ministrations, but I do know that in that dim little shop, with the languorous strokes of the brush, my loneliness disappeared.

No words, no need for them. The whole experience could have been felt as sisterly or as sexy, but actually the ambiance was just friendly. I am embarrassed to admit that at the end I did try to give her a tip. She pushed away my money with a hurt look. It was personal, what she had done for me. I, too, would take nothing now for that memory and feel almost exploitative writing it down for others' eyes. I have never told anyone about this curious incident before. What was to tell really? And yet it stays with me, as does the brush, which I am still using ten years later. When I pick it up each morning, it feels laden with meaning, a kind of heirloom, a daily reminder of the many ways we are all the same, with the same needs for ritual and tenderness past language and culture.

Why I Live Here

Tired and jangled from city imperatives, and perhaps from those of the 1960s themselves, I had agreed to go with some other University of California Berkeley students on a weekend silent retreat to nearby Sonoma County. I knew only that it was scenic, and that we would be near the town of Occidental where people often went to eat epic Italian meals.

I turned up at our departure point burdened with a backpack of books (in case things got dull at the retreat, which they did not), a sleeping bag (in case the blankets were institutionally thin, which they were not), and a box of Oreo cookies (in case the food was inadequate, which it was not). It looked as if I had come prepared for everything except satisfaction.

As we crammed our gear into the cars, everyone seemed to be harboring anxieties about this venture. One of the students whispered to me that she hoped "that priest wouldn't start talking about religious stuff before we even got to the Center," but there was no problem as the dear fellow simply announced that "naps were one of God's good creations" and snoozed most of the drive.

I must have dozed off too, because it was dark outside when I began to pay attention again, or was it that our little procession had entered into the dark woods of my dreams? Brushing gently on both sides of our cars were lacy branches flowing like sleeves, gesturing, drawing us along. The road had become more like a path, our cars slowing out of respect for the curves, but also out of deference to the difference. Everything had changed. The air had become aromatic, earthy, the climate cool and damp, the light suddenly darkness visible. Our pace was slower but with no sudden stops, and even the crowding in the cars came to seem intimate rather than just uncomfortable. Friendly without being familiar, the forest greeted us, made us welcome.

Those mysterious trees swept us along with their angel brooms, until, and it seemed not by our own volition, we were there. The rustic sign, caught momentarily in our auto lights, promised St. Dorothy's Rest. We had missed all of "downtown" Occidental and gotten to the heart of the matter, the old Retreat Center in Camp Meeker, a tiny settlement that loomed large on our maps.

Clambering out of the cars, we had to bend our necks to look up at the still trees. Their huge scale reduced me to a child again; the vow of silence kept us from the need to verbalize so-called adult responses. Free from exclaiming "how beautiful" at every redwood tree, free from subtitles, I internalized those first impressions, making them all the more intense, personal, and memorable.

The memories are still there thirty years later, from domestic details such as the clang of the old-fashioned bell that called us to meetings and meals, to the spiritual rewards of the liturgy in the chapel, which looked like a redwood tree made habitable. I remember too the rewarding logic and clarity of my dreams in my monastic room, which smelled of the incense of many wood fires.

When we took walks on the soft, firm, forest floor, we observed every move of the natural world and did not feel the loss of conversation. At meals we developed a sixth sense, as we could not call down the long table for the breadbasket. People who might have been noisy, boring, irritating in their chatter (me, for instance) became attentive to the needs of others. Silence outside was reflected by silence within. It was not isolating. Cherished we all felt in silent communion with one another and with nature, healed we felt, or at least healing. No one told us what to do, and for the most part I did nothing.

Our allotted time passed pleasantly, although and because nothing much happened: no one got bored, cold, or hungry for Oreos. How often can we make such a claim and mean it? We were as if under a spell cast by those ancient, interlaced trees, rooted in the earth that suited them so well. Balance, was that what we achieved? Something fragile, inarticulate, and yet durable.

Leaving on Sunday afternoon was an ejection from paradise, and yet seeing the rural landscape backwards, in daylight, had its own charms. The place which we had made so our own during the time we spent there would soon be greeting new arrivals with the same impartial graciousness. The redwoods and bay laurel would offer to all that magical invitation to be quiet, to be attentive, to be satisfied, even in a world so beset. To this day, I do not know who St. Dorothy was, and yet I knew by the end of that weekend what Rest was.

By good fortune, several years later I came to live in Sonoma County. Though my "saint" is Sonoma State University, built on the treeless terrain of a former seed farm, there are still redwing blackbirds and jackrabbits, still a sense of rest and of home, and time enough for attentiveness to my inner needs and those of others. Somehow it seemed I had earned the chance to live here because of that quiet reverence informing my first visit.

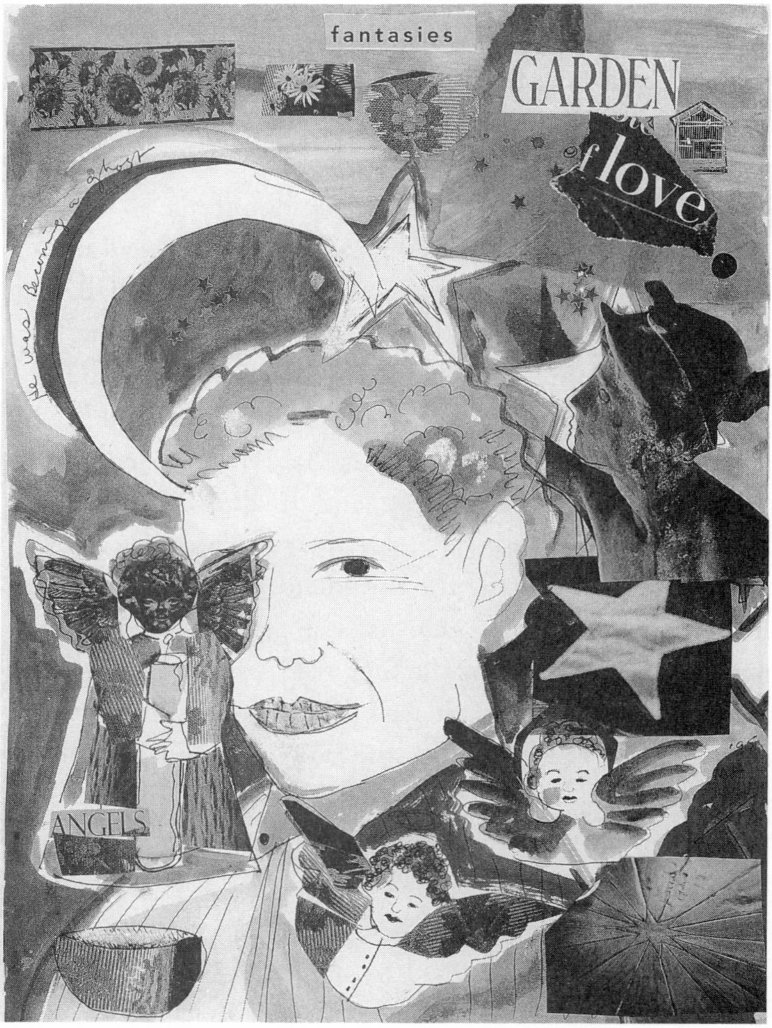
fantasies
GARDEN
of love
He was Becoming a ghost
ANGELS

The Over-Spilling Bazaar

Marylu Downing

Twisting the key hard and shoving open the shop door, Phoebe breathed in the strong aromas of potpourri and old cedar. She smiled. Flipping on the lights, she went over behind the counter and tucked her purse into a place where it couldn't be seen. Despite her love for the shop and her comfort here, she felt uneasy. The money she counted out for the day trembled in her hands.

Phoebe earned the money now. Her shop was barely supporting itself, much less the two of them. She didn't know why she worked so hard and worried so much when Neil never noticed her anymore. Occasionally he looked up from his book or the television, but he didn't really see her; he wasn't there. He was becoming a ghost.

He had quit his job without any explanation. She thought he liked being a carpenter, but he came home early one afternoon and announced that he would never go back. Of course, that gave him more time for the things he really loved. Often he sat very still on the couch reading a paperback novel, smoking roll-your-own cigarettes and drinking vodka mixed with Coke.

At dinner, Neil ate as fast as he could, avoiding her

attempts at conversation. In bed at night, he sometimes cried out and sat up, rocking back and forth. This scared her and she wanted to help him, to keep him from disappearing completely. She had, at one time, loved him. To soothe him, she would place his hand on her breast. Then they'd make love in their usual style, quickly with neither of them making a sound. Words might cause them to break into pieces like the imitation crystal bowl she once dropped. There had been so many tiny fragments of glass from the bowl that for years afterward she found shiny slivers as she vacuumed.

As she sorted through the mail, Phoebe began to relax. It was easier to focus on business than to think about Neil. She sat down at her desk and called New York, reading off numbers from one of the catalogues in front of her. She hung up and dialed another number and then a third. When she finished her orders her stomach was so tight she could barely breathe. It was the moment of regret she always had when she bought merchandise she couldn't afford. She looked around. The shelves of the shop were spilling over. There were piles of clothing on the floor, hats, mobiles and bird cages hanging from the ceiling, jewelry, cards and small antiques coming out of drawers. There were dresses with fairy's wings, rosettes, golden half-moons and silver stars. Burnished wooden chests and dressers held a forest of plaster-cast garden elves, rabbits and frogs. Small boys made of cement held fishing poles and dangled their bare feet over the edges of shelves toward a nonexistent river. Angels cluttered the counter. She could barely clear a space to bag up purchases for the customers, but she didn't mind. She felt secure with the clutter; it meant she mattered.

The next week she had to deal with the jittery suppliers. Retail stores were folding and they wanted reassurance that Phoebe's wouldn't be one of them. They wanted their money.

"Sure," she said to her suppliers, "I'll pay off that last invoice before you ship. How soon can you ship?"

She wondered just how long this could go on. She couldn't stop ordering, and she couldn't pay for what she ordered. But this was before Adorata came in with Phillip and everything changed.

The couple had seen an old wicker rocker outside the shop. It was missing a pillow and had a terrible coat of peeling green paint. That's why Phoebe felt okay about leaving it outside, even though the fog was dripping off the eaves and onto the chair. Adorata and Phillip really wanted the rocker. They tried to talk Phoebe down but she held firm on her price, thinking of the next shipment of goods being trucked to California from the East Coast, imagining herself eagerly ripping open the cartons, smaller boxes full of goods tumbling out onto the floor. Finally, they agreed on a price that pleased them all.

Phoebe thought Adorata and Phillip were the most interesting people she had ever met. Phillip was strikingly tall and solid with a head of red hair. Adorata floated in newly purchased handmade shoes that barely touched the floor.

"Hon, how much is this?" Adorata asked. Phoebe could hardly resist giving her whatever she wanted. Adorata set up an account. Soon the couple had charges and layaways and an ample line of credit given in exchange for the conversation they brought to Phoebe. It was an arrangement they'd all agreed to, without ever really talking about it.

For the Christmas season Phoebe ordered red, green and white lacy things. She ordered small dolls in plaid blankets, flowered enamel boxes, truffles and chocolates in the shapes of reindeer and Santa Claus. For the men she found black hats from Greece. A friend brought in large wreaths made from sage, lavender and bay leaves. The shop began to smell like Christmas, a comforting aroma that, for a few days, made Phoebe feel happy.

As the new items arrived, she had to create new areas to display them. Merchandise began to climb up the walls. Once or twice she thought about the homeless, but soon the sweetness of steaming cinnamon potpourri relegated this guilt to the back of her mind. She went about rearranging, tucking in, fluffing up, and signing charges for Phillip and Adorata.

One day Adorata said to Phoebe, "Hon, why don't I help out for the season? You're busy, and maybe I could work off some of my charges."

Without a second thought Phoebe said, "Sure, sounds okay to me. When do you want to start?"

"Well, right away, 'course."

"What about Phillip?"

"Maybe he could build you some display units."

So that's how it started. Soon Adorata and Phillip were part of the shop. She tried to tell Neil about it, ask his opinion, but he turned away and clicked on the TV. She took this as his way of saying that it was okay.

The following week the marionettes arrived with their long strings and gaping mouths. Phillip mounted a fixture on the ceiling so that the puppets, dangling fiery-colored silk costumes and feathered hats, hung in the air like an ancient Greek chorus.

The sequined vests sold out. The fuzzy bunnies and willow children's chairs went next. Phoebe saw floor and table space she hadn't seen in months. Merchandise moved rapidly out the shop door, customers struggling with overloaded boxes and bags. Phoebe had to reorder flowered bags and ask the neighboring merchants for packing boxes. Maybe, Phoebe thought, this surge of business was due to the skills of the honey-tongued Adorata, the handsome Phillip. She began to have hope that everything would work out.

Late one afternoon after a particularly busy, exhausting day of sales, Phoebe returned home and found her husband passed out, nude, in front of the apartment door. She hadn't noticed how fat he had become. He was too heavy for her to move. She gave up trying to push him toward the apartment door. She couldn't just leave him here, pink flesh for all of her neighbors to see. What was she going to do? She panicked for a moment, and then she thought of Phillip. She looked up his number, dialed, and as the phone rang, she wondered what she would say when he answered.

"Hello."

"Hello, Phillip, this is Phoebe. I need your help," she said, trying to swallow an enormous lump that had formed in the back of her throat.

"What is it, Phoebe, new cabinets, rewiring the display box?"

"Nothing like that. It's . . . it's very personal."

"Where do you live, Phoebe? I'll come over, we'll talk."

"No, it's not talking I need, it's, well, yes, come over."

She gave him her address and hung up.

She opened the apartment door cautiously so she wouldn't hit her husband in the head. He was still comatose, vodka bottle clutched in his hand. She started to think he might be dead. Then she noticed his potbelly slowly rising and falling. For a brief moment she was terribly disappointed. Her hands were sweaty. She felt a headache starting in her left temple. Closing the door she walked over to the couch and sat down, massaging the spot that hurt with the tips of her fingers.

"Whoa, what have we got here?" Phillip's voice boomed, echoing off the thin apartment walls. Why was he so loud? Phoebe wondered. She rushed to the front door before Phillip could say anything else that might attract the neighbors' attention. She tried to nudge the door open. Her husband had rolled against the door, imprisoning her. She was trapped inside her apartment by this embarrassingly naked man who was her husband, her lover, her ghost.

For a moment Phoebe regretted calling Phillip, wished he would just go away. She took a deep breath; a shudder went all the way from her lungs down to the bottom of her feet.

She was able to stick her hand through the small opening between Neil and the door.

"Pretty sight, huh?" she said to Phillip as she pointed toward Neil. "Phillip, meet my husband Neil. Neil, this is Phillip."

Neil missed his part of the introduction.

"You don't think he'll try to hit me or anything if I lift him? You do want me to bring him inside, don't you, Phoebe?"

Phoebe considered what it would be like to see Neil rolling down into the swimming pool at the bottom of their apartment stairs. He would drown, not just because he was drunk, but because he had never learned to swim. He was so terrified of water that he'd glance back over his shoulder when he walked up the steps, just to make sure the pool was where it should be.

"Phillip, I think he's too far gone to punch anybody. Is he too heavy?"

Phillip easily lifted Neil over his shoulder, fireman fashion, pushed open the door to the apartment and asked, "On the couch or on the bed?"

"Bed," Phoebe answered, suddenly embarrassed by her underwear on the floor, her clothes thrown in a pile, Neil's vodka bottles rolling around in the hallway.

As Phillip lowered Neil down onto their bed, her husband's small flaccid penis bounced with the motion. It disgusted her. She started to cry.

"Ah, honey, don't worry, he'll sleep this one off," Phillip said.

She knew what Phillip said was true, but she also knew that there would be more times like this and the thought made her cry even harder. Phillip put one of his big arms around her, brushed back her bangs, and kissed her on the forehead.

"Now, Phoebe, this seems bad, but really, it's going to pass. In fact, someday in the future you and your husband will laugh about this."

Phoebe started to say that she and her husband didn't laugh anymore, but she stopped herself. She didn't want Phillip to feel sorry for her.

"Why don't you come and spend the night with

Adorata and me?"

Phoebe thought about it. She would like to be around the two of them. To have them to herself. Adorata could talk soothingly in that Southern way she had and Phillip could walk around in his underwear. It would be the way she had imagined that she and Neil would always live.

She took a mental inventory. If she went with Phillip, she would get a peaceful night of sleep, a break from Neil. But there was Neil. Who would be there to make sure he was all right, see that he didn't drift off to that place of ghost husbands? Maybe she would never see Neil again. Who would feed the cats and pay the rent and keep things in order? Speaking of order, she needed to talk with Adorata about what needed to be reordered for the store. She thought staying with the couple might be an imposition, and she hated the idea that Phillip might have asked her out of pity. But look what Phillip had just done for her, and he didn't seem embarrassed or pitying; he actually seemed rather jolly about the whole thing.

"Why that's sweet of you, Phillip. Just let me pack a few things."

Phoebe opened her old suitcase and threw in the dress with embroidered sunflowers, a change of underwear, her thin cotton nightie, a toothbrush, and a handful of tampons. God, she hoped she wouldn't get her period tonight. Without looking at herself in the mirror, she caught up her hair in a scrunchie, picked up her purse, took out her key and locked Neil into their apartment.

"You're doing the right thing, Phoebe. Anybody can tell by looking at you that you need a break, need someone to look after you for a change. You work too hard. You should let Adorata and me help more."

Phoebe had wondered at first if Phillip and Adorata were taking advantage of her generosity, but they had become her friends. She didn't know whether to feel relieved or upset. She was not used to someone caring about her.

Phillip was driving with one hand on the wheel, one resting on the back of her seat. His hand was so close to her shoulder that she could feel the heat from it. She imagined him gently touching her. She began to question her decision. She had a fleeting thought of Neil waking in the night and trembling, reaching for her and finding only the nap of the flannel sheet.

"Why, hon, look at you, you've got makeup streaked all over your face." Adorata wiped at Phoebe's face with her apron. "Now, come on in, and we'll have us some tea. Have you eaten supper? Let's just not talk about what happened 'til later."

Phoebe felt her face flushing. She was angry, not at Adorata but at herself. She vowed that this was the last time she would cry over Neil. Turning away, she wiped at her eyes again, just to make sure that all the mascara was gone.

Phoebe was soothed by Adorata's soft tones and by the way she walked so quietly in her colorful leather shoes. "One of a kind," she had told Adorata who had bought them at the shop that first day. She noticed that Adorata's eyes were a beautiful green and that she never stopped moving around, was never still for a minute.

Phoebe saw the cement fisherboys on a bookshelf and the stars pasted upon the ceiling of the guest room where Adorata took her suitcase. She stretched out on top of the Irish blanket she recognized as her favorite from the store, the one with cows and sheep grazing under a golden sun in a sky festooned with old Gaelic sayings. She tucked another lacy pillow under her neck. Overhead, members of the original marionette chorus looked down at her.

"Hi," she said to the puppets, admiring the way Phillip had hung them over the guest bed. She felt a little foolish talking to marionettes, but it looked like they were smiling at her. She wished they would move, dance, call out her name.

When she went out to the kitchen, Adorata was preparing a savory dinner. Garlic, mushrooms, and the faint odor of something chocolate made her hungry. She sat at the table with its familiar centerpiece of angels holding white candles. Phillip rocked slowly back and forth in the green-painted rocker reading the sports page and easily laughing and making comments about the news to no one in particular. He seemed content. She couldn't help comparing him to Neil. The comparison left her bewildered and uncomfortable. She worried about her growing attraction to Phillip. She would never do anything to hurt Adorata, but she would love to sit on Phillip's lap, to have him touch her hair softly like Neil used to do when he was still Neil and not a ghost.

"Hon, could you just put these bowls on the table? They're for the soup."

Adorata handed Phoebe three bowls. They were china, a cross-hatched pattern with floral borders that she recognized from dinners at her grandmother's. Longing for those warm summer nights made her feel like crying again, but she pushed her chair back and walked into Adorata's kitchen. She saw that Adorata had an entire set of the china. She remembered the arguments that her sisters had over who would get Grandma's china. She had let them take almost everything pretty and valuable. Neil and she were vagabonds then with no place in their lives for things like fine china. Anyway, she wasn't sure they would have taken care of it properly. Neil had been known to throw things when he had too much to drink.

For just one moment, Phoebe felt envy for this couple in their cozy home with fancy dishes and gourmet dinners. Holding the china bowls tightly in her hand she looked around carefully. Seeing all of the items from the shop in their home calmed her and made her less jealous. Their home was almost like an extension of the shop, of her. Phoebe was suddenly glad she had come here with Phillip. She found herself softly humming "Heart and Soul," a song she and her friend Lucy had played over and over again on the piano when they were twelve.

Like the stretching of a large animal waking from a nap, Phoebe felt a pushing against the boundaries of her body, against her self. She held up one of the bowls to the light. The translucence was the way you could tell if the china was real. Her grandmother had taught her that. She wasn't thinking of Neil at all as she carefully placed the bowls on the table, rubbing the smooth rim of each one for good luck.

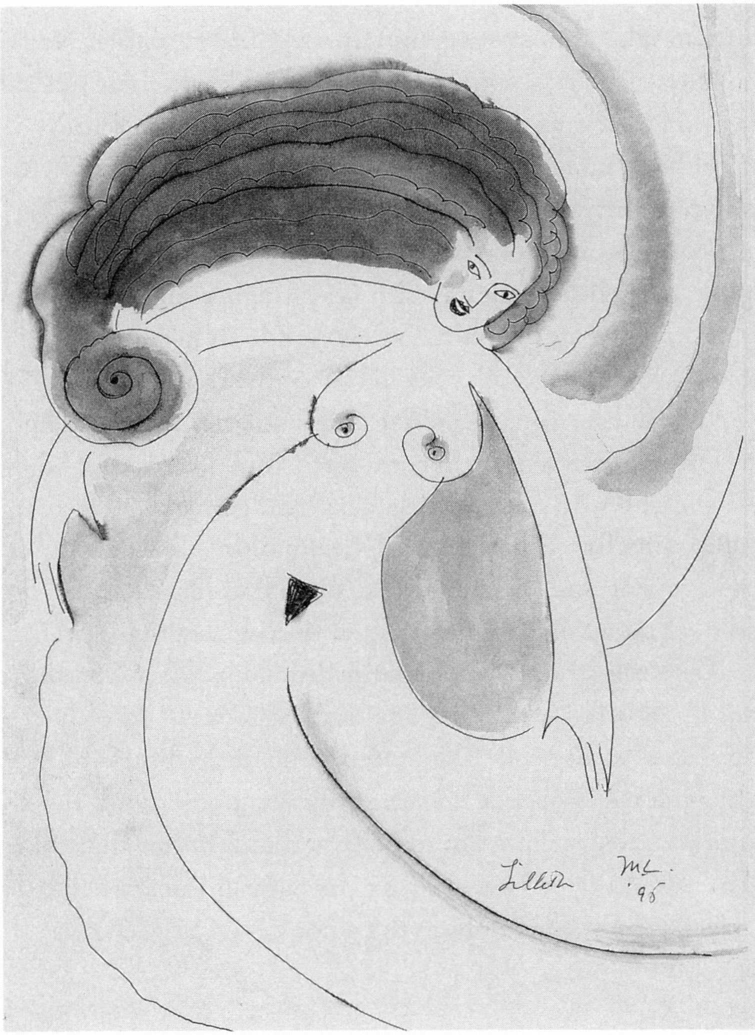
Lilith

Talking with Adam
(Who Never Listens)

Fionna Perkins

Tracking my lineage, I retrace the trail to Eve and the rib story. I can't buy it, Adam. I prefer Lilith as model—your first wife, formed of dust from the four corners of earth, the same as you, Adam, who tore around the planet as your equal and with a temper to match. You clashed, of course, she wanting a dyarchy and you determined to be the first man a king.

Who arranged the divorce? God? I doubt it. He'd just invented birds, and their antics fascinated him. More likely the work of hired scribes rewriting his and her stories, demoting women healers to chambermaids and relegating Lilith to myth and prehistory.

Still, there's no war between us, Adam, except as you make one by turning hostile and combative when I decline to play the roles you choose for me, of underling, of indulgent mother, of fantasy heart-of-gold whore or of victim like poor hapless used and misused Eve.

How you see the rest of us—hoo, boy! What a crew of monsters!

Witches, sirens and snake-headed demons souring

cow pastures, singing sailors to death in inlets of rock and mysteriously draining you and your brethren of vital fluids in the night, and werewolfesses, vampiresses, stalking cats any size anywhere, chimeras, gargoyles and whatever weird being recurs in your worst nightmares—*these are ME?*

If strong or kindly, Adam, you think me odd—*different.* Fierce and protective, a maniac. Perceptive and intelligent, I'm—God forbid—competing! Sensitive, over-emotional, intuitive, practicing the black arts; expressing empathy, mawkish or maudlin.

Wise?—ah, there's the crone—beware the evil she may spread abroad with spells and secret midnight stews of *Amanita pantherina,* newt eyes, grizzly claws and tansy leaves.

So we're back to Eve, whose name in Hebrew means life. What exactly was her sin? She was hungry and ate a prize apple being saved for the county fair? You would know, Adam, if she were already pregnant with Cain. *I'm starving,* she'd say and wanting your get to endure.

Wasn't that what God intended?

Wigs

Cathy - appreciate your appreciation Joyce Griffin

Joyce Griffin

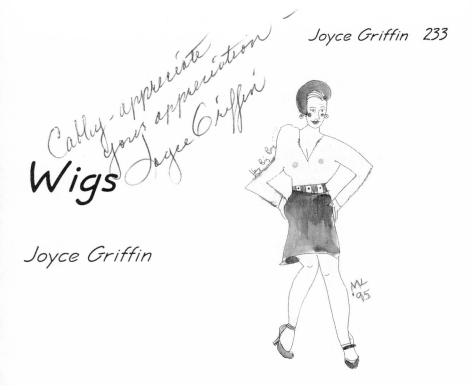

Moira was irritable. The water moratorium case she'd won was being appealed, its final vote by the Board of Supervisors scheduled at the end of the week. Her daughter, Dana, was out with the son of a drug dealer, and Joan Rivers, pushing fifty, was wearing a miniskirt to interview Geraldo on national TV.

Moira recalled that the final *Women's Wear Daily* recently had run a brief, haughty article about the mini-skirt return. "It's economics," the columnist wrote. "It's cheaper. Hemlines always rise during times of war. More money for less fabric, the purchaser pays more for less suit, more design. Production costs go down, since it takes less time to cut and sew, and profits are up." She had pushed herself to finish reading the article that continued for another page, resenting women being held hostage by the Madison Avenue fashion industry.

Moira grew up during the sixties and went through the hippie mini craze herself, so true exploitation she knew from experience. That this shadow was now looming over her daughter's generation was sufficient to send her beyond journaling, back to her writing rage. While her friends, Mamie, Jan, and Lena, were writing Peace in Bosnia letters to their congresspeople and news editors, Moira was writing for Peace Below the Belt. She knew that a more serious correlation existed between short skirts, war and rape, and *Women's Wear* wasn't acknowledging the connection.

She thought she could find her answer by writing. "As skirts rise, so do incidents of rape. . . ." She turned to her keyboard and spent hours searching the Internet for proof of this statement, but the studies she found showed inconclusive evidence. She knew it was more than her own hunch, and wrote from her gut.

"Peace begins at home, the self within. . . ." Moira began another article. Images by a man who thought he knew more than anyone what women look like began to surface. She went with Gauguin's words. He said in 1895, "Women want their liberty. They have a right to it. But they are not prevented from getting it by men. The day they cease to site their virtue below their navels they will be free. And perhaps healthier."

"Insult!" she shrieked at him as though he were standing before her. "You male chauvinist pig artist! A hundred years ago, and you dared blame women for your fallen behaviors! Well, Paul, if you're trying to tell women the crux is in our crotch and it's up to us to get it out, let me tell you, by Gaug, we will."

The issue of the crotch had been bothering her, cropping up in the darnedest places, and then disappearing for a short time only to reappear, forcing itself into even her sleeping hours. Moira began to get up in the middle of the night. Why was she obsessing? Should she see her psychiatrist? Were the mid-calf skirts in her closet markers of a jealous dowager gnawing away at the drumsticks of youth? Surely she was beyond that. Or was she merely anal-retentive while all these young mini-skirted women were oral-relentive, proving they had nothing to hide? Did they have both brains and brash, brains and ass? She rolled these thoughts into a mini worry ball inside her brain and still couldn't squeeze herself to sleep. Why wasn't Dana home yet?

When Moria went to her law office the next morning, a message on her answering machine asked her to address the Tiburon Chamber of Commerce on Thursday about the water rights case she had recently won on a thread. She'd been instrumental in the move to stop cities and highways from spreading across agricultural lands in west Marin, forever. And now the Board of Supervisors, also members of the Chamber, would vote at this meeting whether to support the moratorium.

Skipping over the skirt issue for a while, Moira thought about the water issue and the speech. She phoned the new president of the Tiburon Chamber of Commerce, Susan Wire.

"Susan, I'm thrilled that I'm invited to speak, but I'm a little nervous about the timing."

"Why? I think it's perfect."

"Don't you think it best not to raise any more controversy about the case until Judge Harman has a chance to review it and set calendar?"

"You're not backing out, are you? We invited you because we felt the topic's a vital issue. I don't think it can help your cause if you're hesitant."

"Oh no, no. I appreciate being invited. I'll think of something."

Moira mulled aloud into the phone, "I must think of something powerful, something that would distract those dark-suited sleazoids from the south. They've been flirting their way toward our water, obscuring the critical elements of the case."

"I think you could win the appeal if Judge Harman knew you had the support of the Board of Supervisors. You already have me and, no doubt, Jed," Susan said.

"What if I have a panel of attorneys present different portions of the water project rather than speaking alone?"

"Sure, why not? That would certainly deflect the focus from you."

"Let me think and call you back."

Moira's legal compatriots had rallied round her over the water issue, especially the women in her book club. They'd even chosen WATER as their acronym—Women Attorneys Trans Erotic Read.

Her secretary, Jan Stark, brought a cup of hot coffee and left.

Then into Moira's caffeinated mind popped a sentence from "Striptease," the Roland Barthes essay, "A few particles of eroticism, highlighted by the very situation. . . negates the flesh and . . . plunges it afterward into a permanently immune moral good." What does this mean? Moira wondered. How can I use this concept?

And then it came—her idea for fusing a political

statement about miniskirts with the water vote. All she needed was to try out her plan on her closest women friends.

Jan Stark arranged for six of Moira's colleagues to meet late that afternoon. She warned them that the format was to be personal, intimate, shocking.

Fearless, Jan Stark began. "After all, what woman in the audience hasn't been seduced by a chance to receive a grant in exchange for a night in Mendocino, or a trip to Club Med for working overtime? I remember the time Syd Shek, once National Bank president, tried to get me to fly to Miami to meet him at a conference and I announced it to the associates at the Friday breakfast meeting."

Mamie Bart told her infamous story of nervy Professor Bates asking to touch her breasts as she transcribed his faculty lecture notes. She wrote his question into the transcription, which was distributed throughout the university after his lecture.

"Okay, okay, like most women, we've all had men of power offer a sop in exchange for a romp," Lena summarized.

Moira laid out her plan. "Here are seven triangular shapes I've cut from a black shag bath rug." She held up two samples. "To the back of each I have attached a piece of Velcro with its other part stuck to the outside crotch of each of these new nude panty hose. These are my gift to each of you. Wear them under your daughter's miniskirt next Thursday night with your spikes."

"You mean our fuck shoes?" asked Mindi.

"Anklestrap platforms even better," Moira assured. "Don't forget to show up at the meeting 6:30 sharp. Wait and see what happens."

"Moira, I'm a blond. Couldn't I please have red?" cracked Benni Weaver.

"This is *metaphor*, honey. Everything between your legs appears dark."

"Well, okay, give me the ammunition."

"This is not for the fainthearted," Moira reminded them. "I called Cathy Lewis before calling any of you and told her about the plan. She screamed, 'Do you want to destroy our county?' It took more time than I want to remember, but I convinced her that to save the county is like anything else. Women use what they have to get what they want, and we depend on men's gonads to get it."

"Whoa! That's for sure! Yeah! Don't you know it!" Cheers, acclaims, and laughter came in unison.

That night at home alone, Moira looked at her daughter Dana's miniskirts. She stepped into a purple velour, a real whorehouse color with a full circle flounce, pulled it up past her hips, and cinched it closed. "This feels ghastly," she exclaimed, as she sucked in her tummy and waggled her pubis at the mirror. "Hey, not bad."

Thursday evening the women arrived early for the meeting in the Tiburon High School auditorium. Moria peeked at the audience gathering on the other side of the curtain. Six black-suited men with charts and papers were lined across the front row. "The case is a cinch. What a bother to come out on club night!" Moira heard.

The board sat themselves in the row behind the men. Supervisor Phyllis Jones nodded a kind greeting to Moira. Jed Thomas, also a supporter of the water moratorium, sat with Andy Lipton and Joe Flauder, supporters of spoiling west Marin. Susan Wire stood at the center wearing a blue pleated mini and chatting with Andy and Joe.

At precisely 7:00, Susan Wire climbed to the stage, welcomed the audience, and introduced the panel. Groomed, miniskirted with identical nude stockings, the five women, led by Moira, ascended the stairs like dance queens. Hot breezes and admiring eyes flowed past their exposed legs as they walked in front of the table and then around behind it. Each woman slowly pulled out her chair. Moira removed the protective red modesty skirt from the speaker's table, leaving only the surface cloth.

Jan's red and white silk shimmered like the American flag next to Lena's red and green plaid swishing her dimpled thighs. Mindi's high shiny spikes and black leather mini hugged her like Wonder Woman's costume. Beverly almost cooed in her baby-blue rayon skirt and matching top.

After the introductions, Susan Wire's voice dropped into silence.

Moira stood, then stared down at the men seated below her.

She briefly encapsulated the water story while watching her audience's response. The men were restless, crossing and uncrossing legs, folding arms, leaning slightly forward. They squinted hard, hoping what they thought they might be seeing they were seeing below the tabletop. One loudly gasped, "Oh my God," taking attention away from Moira's speech.

A woman got up and tiptoed over to Susan Wire, "You need to place the cover panel around the speaker's table. They're looking up their skirts."

"They're not," Susan whispered back.

"Oh, yes they are! *Look!"* She insisted on trying to convince Susan, shaking her pointed finger at the dark blotches flashing between leggy flesh on the stage.

Moira imagined the sight: Beverly, uncrossing her chubby, strapped ankles, and spreading her full round knees; Jan, simulating a nervous tick, pressing her hand in her crotch while talking; Mindi, pulling her long slender legs together, pushing the dark fur to prominence. It was a nightclub scene.

"Okay, okay, ssshhh! Just sit down. I'll take care of it." Susan patted at the woman.

Moira chose that moment to rise and walk in front of the table. She spoke clearly, "Gravel mining strips the river aquifer of its natural filter system, destroying fishery habitat and polluting our drinking water. If we limit building, we use less gravel."

She noticed agitation in the front row. A hand to her forehead signaled the panel to begin changing their leg positions—uncrossing, recrossing, spreading. The front row looked distracted.

Moira continued, "Get gravel mining out of rivers and into quarries, now."

Hand to forehead again: Spread those legs easily and slowly. Give them a good look. Now close. Cross. Uncross. Open. Close.

After the last panelist, Susan Wire asked into the microphone, "Is there anyone who can speak to the issue?" She challenged, looking deep into the developers' eyes.

"Wait, wait, I want to present our rebuttal," clamored

a man, fumbling his charts as he stood. The rolls fell in a sloppy heap at his feet. Mumbling, he unfurled them.

"Jim?" she addressed another. Jim seemed hypnotized.

Michael Miklin clutched at his lips as if molding them into form. The other men were plainly lost.

Supervisor Susan Wire then proceeded, "Ladies and gentlemen, we've just had this important case presented before us in cogent, sensible logic. We have to save our county. There is no procedure, nor time, to repeat the argument. We agreed last week at our regular board meeting to call for the question tonight . You've had a chance to speak to the issue, and this is not the place for debate. We've already had that. Is there anyone else?" She paused but a few quick seconds. "I call for the question. Clerk Kinney, will you query the board?"

"Supervisor Wire?"

"Yes."

"Supervisor Flauder?"

"No."

"Supervisor Lipton?"

"No."

"Supervisor Thomas?"

"Yes."

"Supervisor Jones?"

"Yes."

The audience broke into applause.

Moira felt a surge of power below her waist. She shoved her chair from the table, leaped up and received the microphone. She spoke to the front row. "There will be no further destroyers in the open spaces of west Marin." She stepped onto the table, spread her feet and wiggled her pelvis toward her audience as she raised a clenched fist. "If you want more urban sprawl, build it somewhere else."

More applause ended the meeting. People stood waiting for more. As they slouched out, the developers snuck one more look at Moira still on top of the table.

To Cathy – Hope you enjoy this travel story –

TALL CITY OF STEPPED STONE

Mary Gaffney

Mary Gaffney

In two months of traveling through South America, we had hotel reservations for only three places. Machu Picchu was one of them. We'd saved the Lost City of the Incas for the end of our travels. Since we weren't about to squeeze the highlight of our trip into one hectic day as most travelers do, returning to Cuzco in the evening, we'd reserved rooms for my husband Gene, myself, our son Gino, and our friend Mike at the Turista, the only hotel on the heights of Machu Picchu.

Nothing we had read or heard prepared us for the spectacular beauty of the electric train ride from Cuzco, to the place Neruda called "Tall city of stepped stone."

Travelers fall under the spell of the destination and forget the enchantment of the journey.

Shirley MacLaine had used our suite while making her TV special on the area. She probably had larger cocktail parties on the private terrace with misty mountain views, but none happier or sillier. We rolled a joint of coca leaves in toilet paper, an act more symbolic than successful, though we did manage to keep it lit briefly without setting Mike's mustache on fire. We drank to our families and friends, to the surrounding mountains described by Neruda as "blue wind and iron cordilleras," to this fallen empire and those who created it, and to Hiram Bingham, discoverer.

Rain forced us to give up the terrace and the hope of sunset among the ancient secret stones. Neither the food nor service at dinner was as indifferent as tourists sometimes reported. I wasn't certain if that meant the hotel had raised its standards, or if months of eating out had lowered ours.

Showers continued, so we adjourned to our sitting room. I tried to read aloud Pablo Neruda's poem, "The Heights of Machu Picchu," but after the first verse the guys refused to listen. This manly aversion to poetry isn't universal. Neruda won the Nobel Prize for literature in 1971 and is widely revered as a poet in his homeland of Chile. He was powerful in the underground and then during Allende's presidency. Much of his poetry is political, including the piece I tried to read. When we were leaving Machu Picchu, I passed my copy of the poem out the train window to a Canadian woman we'd first met in Argentina. She and her husband had hiked in on the Inca Trail. He was a part of the answer to the question,

"Where have all the hippies gone?" Quite a few of them are in Peru. The woven Peruvian bags that we brought back with us for family were scorned by some as "too hippie," adored by others for the same reason.

We fell asleep at Machu Picchu to the sound of rain. At 5:00 a.m. and at thirty-minute intervals thereafter we awoke to the same sound until we knew the sun had snuck up on us. There would be no moonlight, no sunset, no sunrise among the magical mountains for us, but we were far too intoxicated with what we were experiencing to be disappointed in anything we were not experiencing.

During our first day we explored the city extensively: the Main Temple, the Temple of the Three Windows, the House of the Priest, the Cemetery, the Royal Sector and Tomb, the Temple of the Sun, and the Sundial, about which Neruda wrote, "And on this dial the condor's shadow/ cruises as ravenous as would a pirate ship." And on this dial the Inca tied down a huge golden disk each winter solstice to prevent the sun from escaping. Perhaps this practice dated back to forty days and forty nights of rain or to a time of great darkness. Or maybe it was just Inca insurance.

The Inca worshipped the sun. It is touching to read their rulers' comparison of their God and the Christian God of the invading Spaniards. The Inca king understood Christ and God to be one and agreed that He was great. But his God was greater, the king said, because Christ had died while his Sun God still lived. Christ had been reborn once, but the sun was reborn every day.

The Spaniards never found Machu Picchu, and this knowledge serves as a powerful overture to the drama of the site. Yet, strangely enough, we felt that no human hands could have destroyed the magic of this place. Tearing down buildings and walls wouldn't have been enough. Destroyers would have had to move mountains, rivers and rainbows. As far as is known, the Inca were the only people on earth to worship the rainbow. They lived here with rainbows as close companions. The arcs of color linger still, hanging over the Urubamba River. Three thousand feet below the ridge of Machu Picchu, in a 180-degree turn, sweeps "the torrential silver of the Urubamba."

Our goal for the second day was the dome of Huayna Picchu that looms over the city. The guidebook said the trail to the top was very steep and not for those with vertigo.

"I don't know if I can do this," I told the guys. I looked at the trail through binoculars and felt giddy. "See that narrow land bridge that connects the two mountains? It's so exposed." I passed the binoculars to Mike.

"You can take a Xanax," said Gene.

"I'll fend off the poisonous snakes," said Mike, striking at imaginary creatures with his cane. Snakes were make-believe at the moment, but very real in the area.

"Why are we doing this?" I whined a bit.

"We can't leave here without hiking part of the Inca Trail," Gene said.

Nine-year-old Gino gave me a little pat. "Come on, Mom. If I can do it, you can."

A pamphlet on the Inca Trail from Andy's Tour office in Cuzco included a list of "Necessary Equipment." Below the creatively spelled "Cleanex paper" was "Coca leaves." When we began our assault on Huayna Picchu,

Mike pulled a handful of leaves out of his pocket and asked, "Anyone want some necessary equipment?" He stuffed some in his cheek. Although he never succeeded in getting hold of any lime to help release the narcotic elements of the leaves, he said they had a mildly stimulating effect, similar to caffeine. The rest of us thought they tasted bad enough to have a mildly nauseating effect, so we passed on that "Necessary Equipment."

At the trailhead, we signed our names in the log book. The trail was slippery from the rain, and around the first bend in the path Gino fell. He wasn't hurt nor did he come close to falling into the ultimate void, but we were all reminded of how careful we would have to be.

Further along the trail, terrorist graffiti let us know the *Sendero Luminoso,* the Shining Path guerrillas, had passed this way. No one commented. The thinning mists were letting the sun warm me enough that I requested a brief stop to take off my raincoat and stuff it in Gene's backpack.

"How're you doing?" he asked.

"Great!" I replied. "I'm going to the top."

"I'm not doing so well," he said.

"What's wrong?" I asked in amazement. Gene wasn't afraid of heights or much of anything.

"Mike and I took some acid, and I'm sorta strung out," he said.

I felt a flash of anger. Normally, Gene's physical strength and temperament made him our protector. Now his wimpy wife, young son, and handicapped friend were on their own. My anger burned brighter with the knowledge that I'd have to stifle it. Things should be said to reassure rather than disturb people on drugs. I said,

"You're going to be just fine, darlin'." I didn't want him to freak out on the "awesome spiral way."

I gave his hand a loving little squeeze. My anger disappeared and was replaced with sincere support. Hadn't he seen me patiently through a few anxiety attacks of my own? I told him, "I didn't take a Xanax, but I brought one with me. You can have it if you don't calm down. One way or the other, you'll be okay."

Minutes later he'd hiked his way out of paranoia and begun to climb the steep steps cut into the mountainside. We climbed, Neruda wrote, "flower by flower, through the thickness."

There was no level ground. It was tough going, and we worried about Mike—his artificial hips, his troublesome knees, his entire body. Every few minutes he added a few leaves to the cud he was chewing, like the local Indians do. When the steps and trail were replaced by huge rocks, he cursed. His body breaks more easily than it bends.

We made a plan. Gene helped me up on the rock, then I gave Mike a hand while Gene gave him a boost. He was careful not to push; I was careful not to pull. Either pressure could hurt Mike. We tried to be as steady and strong as the steps and handrail that weren't there. We became the steps and handrail. Once Mike was up on a rock, Gino handed him his cane. "Ha!" said Mike, giving the rock a good whack with the cane.

"Is it much further?" Mike asked two hikers coming down from the top.

"No."

"At least the trail's not difficult," said Mike.

One hiker laughed ruefully. The other said, "It's

worth it."

We continued the trip Neruda described, "Then up the ladder of the earth I climbed/ through the barbed jungle's thickets/ until I reached you, [Huayna] Picchu."

There's nothing at the top but the top. No city or temple. No snack bars or rest rooms. Just the top of the mountain and not much of that, like the pointy peak of a mountain in a child's drawing. We might well have stepped into a drawing, the world was so still and silent, "a new level of silence."

The views of the ruins, the valley, and the Cordillera Vilcabamba are as breathtaking as the hour-and-a-half climb. We saw the multiple switchbacks of the road the buses use. We ate chocolates and drank fruit juice on top of the world.

The woman from Canada we'd met earlier was up there with her husband. They'd been hiking the back side of the mountain looking for the Temple of the Moon, in reality a small cave temple. They hadn't found it. We decided not to leave our perch to join their search, but finally tore ourselves away to return to the hotel before they stopped serving lunch.

Now it was our turn to reassure the few hikers coming the other way that it wasn't much further, and, yes, it was worth it. Merely seeing us may have inspired them. If the little boy and the guy with the cane could make it, then by God, they could too.

The title & all poetry excerpts are from: Pablo Neruda, *The Heights of Machu Picchu,* trans. Nathaniel Tarn. (New York: Farrar, Straus & Giroux, 1966).

Happy reading,
Susan Swartz

A Slightly Dangerous Intersection

Susan Swartz

Katherine Hummer sits in a corner cafe in the old bohemian part of Munich called Schwabing. She is clearly an American. You can tell by the amount of concentration she gives to her *International Herald Tribune.* It's much easier to focus on a newspaper on a sunny Saturday morning if you can't eavesdrop.

Occasionally her ears tune in a word of English and she pauses to listen, but mostly she enjoys the foreign conversation as background music. Her husband, Alfie, a serious-faced man in a hooded burgundy sweatshirt and jeans, is studying the paper across from her.

Katherine spots an item that says Ali MacGraw turns fifty-seven today. This is not something most people would brag about reading in the *Herald Tribune*. Katherine tells friends back in the states that she reads it to keep up with all the wars around her, the latest crime waves in the U.S., and the exchange rate. She is proud to need to know the exchange rate. When you're in California you don't care about that day's value of the American dollar.

But when you are in Munich and thinking it would be nice the first long spring weekend to jump on a train and go into Italy, then you give it a thought. It's the same little bit of money in her life which now multiplies nicely into lira and divides rather brutally against the mark.

Katherine is smug about knowing these things. She sometimes imagines there is a life censor checking on the class of 1963, El Cerrito High, who beams her up periodically. Right now, he's saying, "Oh wow, look at where our Kate is today. She didn't get those shoes at the Pleasant Ridge Mall."

The *Tribune* is for Americans abroad who, because they are away from Topeka or Sacramento, need to know things about the world that they probably wouldn't bother with when hunkered over their Grape Nut Flakes back home.

But the *Tribune* isn't stupid. Its editors know that the most sophisticated readers still like a gossipy element with their breakfast. Katherine certainly knows this. She used to write entertainment news for a newspaper, more of the Topeka variety than the *Tribune,* but as she says to Fanny, her sister, "They're all the same except the big ones put Mother Teresa in their people columns. The small ones only have room for Julia Roberts."

Well, well, look at this. Ali MacGraw is fifty-seven. Katherine realizes that this fact makes her feel suddenly happy. Now she needs to figure out why. She looks up from the paper and sticks her tongue down into her café au lait. This is another thing about Europe, that you can drink coffee like a cat. Is it tastier? No. And sipping hot liquid out of a bowl that requires two hands to lift is hardly efficient.

Actually it cools faster than in a mug. But the image is attractive, like sashaying your knife and fork together, stabbing the food with your left hand.

Perhaps there is comfort in knowing that Ali MacGraw is fifty-seven because she still looks like Ali MacGraw. What does that mean? She still looks like someone Katherine, just peeking into fifty, would like to look like. Which means it's possible to be fifty-seven and inspire envy in others.

God, is that what it's about? Well yes, in many ways, shallowly speaking, it is. Because if you don't inspire envy in others, then you might inspire pity. Or be ignored altogether and go through life creating barely a stir.

Katherine sometimes wonders if what she wants is to inspire envy more than respect. Now, that's some admission for a woman of the nineties. She might stop the waitress and ask her if she wonders the same. Would she rather have people covet her youth, her shiny tan legs in black hiking boots, over her greatness as a human being? She could attempt this since all German waitresses, at least those under thirty, speak English. But the young woman might walk off saucily, clearly leaving the message, "Envy this, mother."

There is something about young good-looking Germans. They're aloof and confident. They don't go around grinning like American youth, pretending to be congenial. The Germans hold back. Alfie says they're conversational but they don't kiss up, and Katherine knows he admires their restraint. Today he probably also admires the way the waitress' expensive leather skirt lies flat as a pan across her stomach.

Katherine and Alfie have impressed the waitress here

by telling her they are from California. Germans continue to fantasize about California. They travel to the United States but usually get no farther than Florida. They see Disney World, swim in the Atlantic in February, and don't approach the other coast. So the California mystique of utter hipness remains intact. Katherine has allowed everyone she's met here to think she lives in San Francisco, although she's a couple of suburbs north.

"Fifty-seven years should have given her enough time to learn how to act," Alfie would say were she to report the birthday news. The other night they'd watched one of those overdone World War II epics, the one Ali MacGraw was in before they replaced her with the British actress with the long hair.

"Geez, she's an embarrassment," Alfie said, and Katherine rolled her eyes as if in agreement.

"People used to say I looked like her." Alfie's nod tells her she's told him this several times before.

She also was told in junior high she looked like Natalie Wood and once, when she got a shag haircut, her first husband kidded that she was trying to do a Jane Fonda. This gives an idea how long ago Katherine could boast a slight resemblance to Jane.

She enjoyed being compared to the actresses, but not just because they were pretty. They played women who back then represented a new style of self-confidence. They were bold and daring. Even the gentle and lovely Natalie let you know she had appetites.

Katherine went to all their movies, even the worst of Ali's. She took comfort in the fact that her contemporaries were doing well. As long as they continued to thrive and look terrific in the process, so might Katherine, their younger mirror image.

It was a failing, she told her sister, that she ended up with such narrow role models.

"I should aim toward someone like Pat Schroeder. God, how I wish I could get worked up over Barbara Mikulski."

Then Natalie drowned. Jane had her breasts done, gave up lefty politics and married that odd Ted Turner. Ali, in terms of acting, never got any better or worse. But there are pictures of her on the back of Steve McQueen's motorcycle that suggest a latent wild woman. As she got older she retained a certain flash, showing up on talk shows, in a black sequined hat, to push for animal rights.

Alfie won't know any of this, won't care and would laugh at Kate for filling her head with such junk. Alfie's head truly is full of Bosnia-Herzegovina. And Rwanda. Lately, Chechnya. When they travel they always share one *International Herald Tribune.* He takes the world news as his responsibility. She gets the rest. Once he broke up a dinner party by asking, "Who the hell is Martha Stewart?" proving he doesn't get into the home and garden pages.

The *Tribune* doesn't divide as easily as fatter papers, but Katherine has learned to break it apart like a cookie. She takes the lighter filling and passes the serious ends to Alfie.

As usual he is scowling at the front page. Feeling what he calls her "nagging eyes," he looks up and asks, "What?" He does not like to be interrupted in the middle of a war.

What she's been thinking is that the holistic Ali MacGraw might possibly be sneaking estrogen into her system.

At Cafe Schwabing three streets come together. Plus two tram lines, three buses and a bike route. Katherine sits there and feels she is in the middle of something.

The waitress says that people are crazy to sit this close to the street. So much traffic. And fumes.

"Is it dangerous to sit here, then?" asks Katherine.

"Not usually," says the waitress, pointing out that their feet are in the bike-path part of the sidewalk.

Suddenly Alfie bursts out, "I don't see how we can possibly continue like this," squeezing his eyes shut and then slowly shaking his head back and forth. Katherine's head snaps up and her stomach starts to tighten.

"Look at this," he says and shoves the front page at her. There she sees a picture of Serb soldiers standing with guns at a checkpoint into Sarajevo. They are threatening to shoot down United Nation helicopters.

Katherine almost smiles with relief. Sarajevo was under attack, not her.

Alfie gets so worked up about world events. He's been tracking the war in Bosnia ever since it began. One day he brought home a picture of the bridge at Mostar, an ancient structure that the Serb rebels had blown to little pieces. He had tears in his eyes.

He cares so much. He knows so much. He wants to be part of it so much.

It's enough for Katherine to be part of a sidewalk scene halfway around the world from where she started. She fears, however, that if a Red Cross jeep pulled up at the curb at this moment and the driver asked if anyone wanted to leave their coffee and come along to Sarajevo, Alfie would be gone.

Katherine and Alfie are bleeding-heart liberals. They are card-carrying Democrats, members of NOW and Amnesty International. They believe in feminism and have marched against war. They are sixties people. They are also fifties children, and so a small and hidden, but controlling, part of them believes that boys have to be brave and girls have to be beautiful.

Alfie regretted not having gone to Vietnam. He went to college instead, which got him out of fighting and into an advertising career. He was grateful at the time, but lately he acts like he blew a pivotal opportunity.

It's not that he wants to be Rambo and take on the Serbs, but Katherine can tell he yearns to be inside the news photographs, that some days he would trade places with the men cutting tree stumps in the Sarajevo parks for firewood.

Katherine tells friends that the only woman she thinks could take Alfie away is Christiane Amanpour, the fearless CNN reporter who acts like she's never met a world disaster she didn't relish.

Katherine's foreign experience is the produce stand across the street, where an Italian couple sells avocadoes from Israel and cherry tomatoes from the Canary Islands. They will be in the tales she takes home. So will the building down the street where Eva Braun once lived, now home to a boutique that sells Patagonia camping clothes.

If Alfie were to go to Sarajevo, she doubts he would return. Not because he'd be killed, although that certainly could happen. Civilians were picked off all the time by snipers, just for crossing the street.

If Alfie were to go to war, he wouldn't return because he would be having too much fun. Someday she will tell him she knows this. But not now.

He takes off his glasses, folds his part of the paper and waves it at her.

"Ready to trade?"

"Sure," she says. "Want to go rent a motorcycle?"

Camel's Hair Coat

Sara Peyton

"Isn't the full moon lovely tonight?" asked Joan, staring intently ahead at the road. Her hands, hidden by black leather gloves, gripped the steering wheel.

"Yes, absolutely gorgeous. It looks just like a silver dollar," replied her daughter. Kate lived in San Francisco and was visiting her mother in Maine. It was below zero outside. Kate shivered and sunk deeper into the heavy camel's hair coat she had found in her mother's closet. Kate was certain the coat had once belonged to her, but her mother said no. Still, the texture of the scratchy wool against her chin felt familiar.

"I'll turn the heat up," Joan said, glancing at her daughter. She wore an oatmeal-colored sweater Kate had given her. The wool was hand-spun and soft, with a sheen almost like silk. "I guess I'm used to the cold."

"I forgot to mention how much I love your new car," responded Kate, trying to sound friendly. Mother and daughter were off to an antique auction. The road was narrow and icy but Joan drove fast, shifting the red mini-van harshly, as if they were late, but there was plenty of time.

Maine was Kate's newly adopted childhood state. Eight years ago, her mother and stepfather had retired and moved from Connecticut to a tiny Maine town named Paris. It was a perfect home town, Kate told her San Francisco friends, with rambling farmhouses, a brick schoolhouse, and a few churches that closed in the summer because of poor attendance.

Kate's two sons also loved Paris. Her husband, a native Californian, admitted he liked Paris too. It had been easy for Kate to sweep her childhood memories out of Connecticut and into Maine. The cozy Connecticut she once cherished had disappeared into a maze of housing tracts, crowded highways, shopping malls, and fast food restaurants. But during visits to Paris, Kate was delighted to splash in what looked like her childhood favorite brook and swing on a twin of her old backyard's climbing tree.

"Memories only in my head don't help me. Things have to exist. They must have a place, so we can taste, smell, see, and touch them when we need them," Kate told her husband. Bill was a programmer working in artificial intelligence, devoted to creating abstract equations out of the smallest details of everyday life.

"I see. It doesn't matter which brook we hear, only that one babbles for us now," said Bill. Her husband had no ear for poetry, but, after her explanation, he no longer complained when Kate told their sons about beloved trails through the woods and lush blueberry patches she remembered from her newly acquired youth in Paris, Maine.

"This has been a wonderful visit, Kate," said Joan, downshifting abruptly and causing the van's front wheels to slide off to the right. "I'm glad we've had so much time alone."

"Me too," said Kate, although she wasn't sure exactly what her mother meant. She did feel nervous about her mother's driving. It was even worse than usual.

Today the boys and Bill had spent most of the afternoon sledding down the big slippery hill behind the house. Kate joined them briefly and crazily sped down the slope, twisting and turning in the green, plastic flying saucer. No fear, she told herself.

Earlier in the day, Kate and her mother had taken down the Christmas tree and carefully wrapped dozens of antique ornaments in tissue paper. The boys had declared their grandmother's glittering tree was the prettiest they'd ever seen. But they were surprised to see the tree still up in late January.

"I kept this room extra cold to keep the tree fresh for you. I so wanted you to see what your mother's Christmas tree looked like when she was a little girl," Joan explained to her grandsons.

"That's right. Mom never allowed us to hang these ornaments on the tree. But we didn't mind because we didn't want to break them," said Kate, adding another fact to her mother's story.

Actually, the faded, hand-blown Santas and delicate frosted-glass pine cones weren't part of Kate's childhood. When her mother was still married to Kate's father, the family tree was decorated with homemade paper chains, pipe-cleaner angels, and clumps of tinsel hung in bunches by Kate and her two younger sisters.

"Your children are lovely, dear," Joan said loudly, taking a sharp turn to the right and bouncing Kate out of her reverie.

"Thanks. I think they're enjoying the year. They like their teachers."

"And how's waitressing?"

"Mom, I'm not a waitress. I own the restaurant," said Kate, not trying to hide her annoyance. Kate knew she was a disappointment to her mother, who, at various times, had wanted her daughter to become a doctor, lawyer, pianist, architect, and once, oddly, a talk show host. In truth, Kate had also dreamed about those occupations, with the exception of interviewing mothers-who-hate-their-daughters on TV, but they remained only fantasies.

Kate's gift was seizing opportunities. The small restaurant she now owned had literally fallen into her lap when the woman she worked for had decided to retire and couldn't sell the business.

"I know you own the restaurant, but I thought you said you were glad for a chance to get away because you were tired from waitressing. Didn't you say your feet hurt or did I just imagine it like everything else I imagined you said?"

This exchange was slippery. It hurt. For a few seconds Kate thought about punching her mother in the face. No one would ever know what caused the accident—the red van lying on its side, the two women tossed together chest-to-chest, dead.

Kate felt the return of a stabbing pain in her stomach. She imagined pointing to her belly, and saying, "Kiss me right here, make it better, please, Mommy." Now that was really sick. Besides, her mother rarely kissed anyone, not even her grandsons. Instead, she pecked at the air, like a lost bird, and hugged so quickly it felt more like getting pushed away than embraced.

"You're right, Mom, I was tired from waiting on tables and I did tell you about it. I'm a little short-handed right now, that's all. Usually I don't waitress."

Her mother smiled. This was what she wanted. She wanted Kate to agree with her, over and over again, many, many times. It was an obsession and very annoying. Often Kate dodged conversation, not to sidestep arguments but to avoid becoming trapped in affirmative gestures; in nodding, *yes, oh yes, of course, I know, you're right, I'd have done the same, what a good move.*

There was one unwritten rule. Kate asked very few questions of her mother because too many might lead to the big question that was never answered: there was still no explanation as to why her mother had abandoned her three daughters almost thirty years ago, only to claim them back two years later with a new husband. Kate's father was only too happy to return them. The girls had quickly learned not to mention what they had done or felt during their mother's two-year absence. Eventually they almost forgot about the absence. Family finances picked up with the new husband. That was something.

Kate ventured a single question, "Mom, why don't you come visit me in California this summer? You can eat at my restaurant and I would be happy to wait on you."

"Dear, you know I don't fly anymore. Unlike you, I'm afraid to fly. Of course, I'm not sure you would visit me if I didn't help out with the cost of the expenses," Joan said. "I guess it would be less expensive if I visited you."

Kate stared at her mother. Her silvery hair looked thick and lustrous in the moonlight. But she seemed changed, even more abrasive than usual. And she had developed a crop of new allergies to soaps and detergents, perfumes, all her silver jewelry, house dust, and dog hair. She was becoming fearful—afraid to fly, unable to sleep alone at night, uneasy in an unlocked house even during the day. She refused to go for regular checkups. "No news is good news," she had said this morning. "Doctors killed your grandfather, you know."

"Mom, do you know that technically we're both middle-aged? Demographically, we're in the same group, even though you're sixty-two and I'm forty."

"Kate, I know you're not a waitress. I don't know why I said that. I'm just so proud of you I guess I'm a little jealous."

There it was. The unexpected compliment, oddly out of place and mostly out of character. Kate really began to feel nervous. The car thumped loudly as they sped over a bump in the road, reminding Kate of the sound of ice cracking in a frozen lake. The air felt thinner and Kate inhaled deeply. It was so dry and cold that Kate wondered if there was less oxygen than usual, like at high altitudes.

Now her mother turned sharply left and the car skidded into a driveway. They had reached their destination. The auction parking lot was almost full and it took a few minutes to find a place to park. When the car stopped, Kate turned to face her mother.

"Mom, what's bothering you?" Kate asked with the suspicion she knew the answer.

Her mother turned and looked at her, her upper lip quivering, "It's a lump, dear. It's probably nothing. I don't want to go to the doctor."

For a moment Kate felt irrational and blinked quickly when she thought she saw her mother's face dissolve into particles of dust. The emotional distance between them was so great. Now, suddenly, they were rushing toward each other with the speed of light, about to collide, maybe explode.

"You're right, Mom. There's probably nothing to worry about. But we're going to have to find out. I can help you. Is it a lump in your breast?"

"Yes." Her mother slowly removed the black leather gloves. Kate sat quietly, unsure what to do next. Without warning, her mother quickly raised the thick, knitted sweater, first above her belly, then above her chest. She drew up her turtleneck shirt, reached behind her back, unhooked her bra, and tucked it above the rolled-up clothing.

In the full moonlight, it wasn't hard to see her mother's skin. Kate stared at the bunched clothing, her mother's pale breasts and dark nipples. She felt she was staring into a mirror. She had never known how similar their breasts looked. Kate searched her mother's eyes.

Her mother touched a spot slightly above her right nipple. "It's probably nothing to worry about. I'm not sure it even is a lump."

Kate reached toward her mother, resting her hand briefly on her mother's fingers. Then she gently pushed her mother's hand aside and lightly felt the outline of a single, hard, almond-sized lump. "When did you first notice this, Mom?"

"Not too long ago. Before Christmas."

"We'll see the doctor tomorrow, Mom. I'll go with you."

Her mother's skin felt warm and satiny. Outside the frigid terrain was all sharp contrast, a brilliant, solid moon above a glazed, snowy surface—the stars, shards of light in the black, unbending sky. Inside the van the air felt dense and muddy. Kate stretched out her arms, pulled her mother close, and hugged her. Her mother's bare flesh pressed hard against the camel's hair coat. The rough old collar rubbed against Kate's chin.

Cathy Hawkins

Simone Wilson

Exposures

Simone Wilson

Kate sat on the redwood stump at the end of the school yard dusting her camera with her grandfather's shaving brush. The school grounds, perched on a sunny hillside overlooking the Russian River, were chalky dry by the end of May. Redwoods grew on the opposite ridge; down below, vineyards in parallel rows ended at the line of willows by the water.

Kate fogged the lens with hot breath and carefully cleaned it with her shirttail. She gave the viewfinder extra attention with the soft bristles and then twirled the focus ring to expose any grit under the mechanism. She couldn't fiddle with apertures or shutter speeds on the old Agfa, just squint and twist the focus ring until the image sharpened. The camera had a nice heft to it, though, and it was screwed into a tight-fitting case of dark leather that her grandfather had handled until it was resilient and smooth.

She shook the brush and blew through the bristles until they fanned out clean, then dropped the brush back into her shirt pocket. It had an ivory handle and pig bristles, and she wondered when her grandfather had ever used it. She remembered him with a beard, not clean-shaven like her Uncle Phil who ran the tackle shop and hardware store, or her dad who had died in an accident up on Meyers Grade Road when she was seven.

Kate surveyed the valley with her camera, then turned and focused on a clump of students in the shade of the bay tree by the long porch. She had her assignment: to take photos of "student life" for the yearbook. Kate was mystified by the alchemy that folded some kids into groups and kept others out. Her cousin Cindy there was always part of a happy cluster, a stable atom in a harmonious molecule. There must be some centrifugal force Kate couldn't grasp, a gravity that pulled some kids in and flung others to the fringe of the galaxy.

Kate was class of '77, still a junior, but in a country school with 200 kids everyone knew everyone else from grade school. Cindy was standing next to Paul Letterman, whose dad owned the theatre in Guerneville; Paul had taken Kate to several pictures when they were fourteen or fifteen. With their sneakers sticking to the floor, they sat in the cool darkness on Oldies Nite, attempting to kiss while Audrey Hepburn danced around Paris with Fred Astaire. Kate didn't remember the plot. She only recalled that her interest in Fred and Paul had fizzled at roughly the same moment, and that by the end of the picture she knew that Audrey Hepburn was the most adorable person in the world.

Kate panned away from the group and focused on Janice Isaacson sitting at the end of the porch, her feet propped on the railing while she tossed up Cheetos and caught them in her mouth. The light was all wrong—Janice was mostly shaded by the porch roof but her arm, stretched along the railing, was in full sun, and so were her sneakers and the cuffs of her tight white jeans. Janice had rolled up the sleeves of her yellow cotton shirt, and her arm, resting on the redwood plank, glowed with a deep tan accented by a silver bracelet. Kate noticed how graceful her wrist looked. She wished she had a zoom lens. Janice tossed the last Cheeto to a sparrow and leaned back, eyes closed. Her blouse riffled slightly as she breathed. Kate became mesmerized by the rhythmic movement of yellow cloth.

Suddenly her field of view became a blur of pale blue. Larry Stoltz's shirt was parked in front of the lens, blocking her perfect view of Janice. "Miz Brit wants the film as soon as you're done," said Larry, "so she can send all the rolls to Santa Rosa at the same time."

"Then get outta my way. She doesn't want pix of your shirt." She and Larry had been buddies since fourth grade and had perfected the art of giving each other a bad time. Kate took a picture of Larry's killer smile, then finished the roll with two of Janice asleep on the porch, lighting or no lighting.

Later that afternoon Kate headed toward the coast in her uncle's delivery truck, which was really just a VW wagon with peeling yellow paint and a couple of two-by-fours bolted to the roof—something to lash pipes to so they wouldn't fly into the road and scare nervous tourists into the river.

Today she had a load of PVC for Eileen Mullins, a rancher out near Jenner who needed irrigation pipes for her garden. The PVC stuck out over the hood and Kate saw the quivering white tubes boing up and down whenever her wheel dropped into a pothole. She passed DeCarly's store, decided to stop for coffee on the way back, and kept heading west past sagging barns and hills flecked with sheep.

After a few miles, the valley widened out to low hills as the Russian River made its final dash for the sea. She crossed the bridge over the river, then turned down a side road through stunted pines and cypresses, heading toward the Mullins ranch. As she came around a blind curve a yellow dog bounded across the road. Kate jerked the wheel to the right and felt a light bump as the dog bounced off the left fender, then a jolt as the right front wheel jammed into a drainage ditch and the car slammed to a stop.

"Shit!" Kate popped the seat belt and jumped from the VW, angry and shaken. The wheel, wedged in the ditch, might be all right. The dog was not. He got to his feet and then spun back down into the dirt with a yelp.

"You okay, fella?" Kate asked softly. She extended her hand hesitantly; even a friendly dog might snap if injured. She could see now he was not full grown—maybe seven or eight months of yellow lab puppy. His big tongue lapped her hand a few times and his tail thumped the dust into little clouds. Maybe he wasn't badly hurt.

Kate opened the back of the VW and lifted him inside, leaving the hatch up. If he felt strong enough to jump out, good. If not, he would have shade and air until she got back. Kate walked down the road to the two cabins—converted chicken coops really—that were the only houses nearby. One looked deserted. An old blue Studebaker was parked next to it; the hood was missing and blackberry vines choked the engine block. A sturdy

1950 vintage Ford pickup was parked by the other one; a small silver Volvo sat next to it. Kate spotted a sack of fertilizer in the truck bed, along with several stacks of the *Russian River News* bound up in twine and left to crinkle up in fog and sun. Inside the cab, mice had helped themselves to some upholstery. Outside, the navy blue paint had worn thin but the tires looked new. She could probably drive this one, maybe even use it to haul a VW out of a ditch.

The deck came into view as Kate crunched down a driveway bordered with nasturtiums. Pots of geraniums lined the deck, and on a redwood table several leathery teabags had curled in the sun next to a chipped teacup. A cricket floated, lifeless, in a dog's ceramic water bowl. A woman lay asleep in a green canvas chair, her feet propped on two more stacks of old newspapers. Kate, who hated waking people up, deliberately ground the gravel under her sneakers to make noise.

The woman looked about thirty-five, with grey sneaking into her short wavy brown hair. She wore cutoff jeans and a light pullover sweater with the sleeves pushed past her elbows. She looked up drowsily as Kate stepped onto the weathered deck.

"Yes?" the woman said, a bit bewildered.

"I'm afraid I hit your dog. A yellow lab, half grown?" Kate felt like an idiot. "My name is Kate."

"Yes, he's mine." She waved a hand vaguely in her own direction. "I'm Gloria Adams."

"I think he's okay. I mean, he's not badly hurt but he should go to a vet. There's one in Guerneville. We could look up his number."

"I don't have a phone," Gloria said wearily. "Could

you take him? I'm not feeling all that great." Kate wondered if she could be this dopey just from snoozing in the sun.

"I think my car is worse off than your dog. It's stuck, anyway."

"Listen, why don't you take him in the truck, and when you get back from the vet you can try to pull your car out. The keys are on the table inside."

This seemed simple, although alarmingly trusting, so Kate opened the screen door and walked into the house. It was one room with bare wooden walls, a stove and sink on one side by a window and a big floppy couch on the other. Kate saw copies of *Modern Photography* on a round oak table, along with more unwashed teacups and a cache of medicine bottles. The keys lay next to a jar of honey. Kate eased the one stamped FORD off the ring and went back outside. "I'll pay for the vet," Kate said, hoping she could afford it.

"No, no, Skipper charges off at every sound. He probably ran into *you*. Let's see how he is, and how your car is, and then we'll figure it out." She looked like she might drop off to sleep again, so Kate fired up the truck and drove slowly up the driveway to rescue Skipper.

At 5 p.m. she lugged the dopey puppy down the gravel path and settled him on the deck. Gloria still sat in the canvas chair, but now she held a Nikon with the widest lens Kate had ever seen. She leaned over and fussed with the dog. "Good boy, stupid old Skipper," she said, rubbing his pink belly. His tail thumped the deck.

"The vet said he's just bruised. He gave me some tranquilizers so he won't run around much for a few days."

"That's great," said Gloria. She looked more alert now.

"Amazing lens," said Kate. "A 500?"

"A 400. You interested in cameras?"

"Oh yeah. I've never seen one like that except in magazines."

"Why don't you take the truck and rescue your car and then come back and look at the camera?"

"Great," said Kate. "If it starts up, I have to leave some PVC down at the end of the road. Then I'll come back." She liked it that the older woman assumed she could get her VW out by herself. Gloria must be one of those capable people who figured other people could do things too.

Kate maneuvered the big blue pickup behind the VW and set the brake. She took a coil of thick, scratchy rope from the back of the wagon; with a couple of half-hitches she secured it to the ball welded on the back of the Ford. The other end went through a metal loop near the rear bumper. Fortunately the load of PVC didn't weigh much extra. Back in the cab, Kate chugged the truck slowly ahead and the VW came out of the ditch with a bump.

Kate started up the VW and drove it hesitantly to the Mullins place. Eileen's car was gone, so Kate unloaded the PVC by the garden while the cats groomed themselves on the hood of the car. Then she curled the car into a Y-turn and drove back to the cabins.

"Everything okay?" asked Gloria when Kate returned in the truck.

Kate nodded. "What a relief. It's my uncle's wagon. I deliver stuff for him."

"So, you know how to hold a camera like this?"

"Left hand under the lens, near the base," Kate answered.

"Yeah, but with a lens this long you want to extend your left hand farther out, so it balances. Use your right hand to steady the camera end of it."

"Whew, it's heavy," Kate said, handing it back.

"Yeah, I have to use a tripod or else rest the lens on something to get a really crisp shot. Since I got here three weeks ago, I discovered I could use the railing. Got some good shots of blue herons the other morning. They're such good boys—they stand still while you mess with lighting and focus."

Kate aimed the cannon-like lens at the town across the river. Blue houses leapt toward her and she could read the lettering on the Jenner schoolhouse.

"Not the easiest thing to walk around with, though," admitted Gloria. "I usually fall back on this one instead." She twisted lens and camera in opposite directions until they separated with a click. She carefully lowered the long black tube into a padded bag and brought out a slimmer lens that she snicked into place.

"This is an 80 to 200 zoom—light enough to hold steady." She passed it back to Kate, who took aim at the town, at Penny Island in the river down below, at a redtail hawk perched on a knob of serpentine. Kate slid the sheath to the end of the lens for a wider view, then eased it back to draw the hawk in closer.

"My camera's prehistoric—an old Agfa with zero settings," Kate confessed.

"No, no. They're good little cameras," Gloria told her. "They just don't let you make any choices. What do you like to take pictures of?"

Kate shrugged, feeling a little shy for the first time. "Horses, especially colts. And kids at school."

"You're in school?"

"Sure, River High. I'll be a senior next year. You a professional photographer?"

Gloria nodded. "For a newspaper in Denver. Do the kids like it when you take their picture?"

"Yeah, but they change when they see the camera. It's better when they don't see me. I need a telephoto so I can be farther away."

"I used to think that too," said Gloria. "You have to learn to get people's confidence so they relax around you. Otherwise you're a voyeur."

"A what?"

"A voyeur—somebody who watches without being involved," said Gloria.

Kate turned away and surveyed the landscape. "You sure look a lot better than you did when I first came down here. I saw the bottles of pills. Are you sick or something?"

"Not sick. Recovering, maybe. They're vitamins mostly, and a little stash of Valium," Gloria said. "A friend died—my best friend, Carrie. After that I didn't know what to focus on. Spoken like a photographer, huh? So I decided to come out here for a few weeks. Make everything simple—eat and sleep and shoot birds and sunsets. Pretty good sunsets from Goat Rock. Why do they call it that? The rock isn't shaped like a goat."

"Actually, it looks more like a meatloaf," said Kate. "I guess they used to graze goats out there."

"I guess," Kate said, wondering if Gloria had deliberately changed the subject. She wasn't used to adults being so frank with her.

"Your friend died and you got depressed," said Kate. "She lived here, didn't she?"

"Did you know her?"

"No, but somebody's been here awhile, to plant the flowers and pile up so many newspapers."

"Maybe you'll be a detective instead of a photographer," said Gloria. "Carrie and I used to share a house in Denver. She moved out here a couple of years ago. I didn't see her after that. Then she got sick—cancer. Friends called to tell me what happened. I needed to see where she had lived, to say goodbye, or something. So I drove out with Skipper."

They sat on the deck, watching the river while the sun went lower.

"Is the water really flowing uphill," Gloria asked finally, "or is that an optical delusion?"

"It's the tide coming in. This time of year the tides are stronger than the river, and they push the water upstream. Funny, huh?"

"Yeah," Gloria said. She sounded genuinely interested. Kate felt a surge of confidence at being able to explain this simple local occurrence and realized she felt more adult at this moment than she had before in her life.

"Well, I have to get the VW back to my uncle and get myself home for supper," said Kate. "Shall I come back and see if Skipper's okay?"

"Sure. He seems all right—he's grounded for the moment, anyway. Bring your dinosaur Agfa, and we'll have a look at it."

Kate visited after her deliveries the next week. She and Gloria surveyed the river while Skipper panted on the deck. Later, they walked through the brush down to the beach and climbed back on the path through the cypress trees. Gloria told Kate about life in Colorado, about a summer house she and Carrie had shared near Boulder, about taking a leave from the Denver paper to work in France after Carrie moved to California.

Kate drove out again the following Tuesday afternoon when there were no deliveries at all and her uncle didn't need the wagon. The fog had burned away at noon. Kate coasted slowly down the dirt road, but the tires kicked up so much dust she had to roll the window shut. By the time she reached the gravel driveway, the inside of the car was a steam bath and she felt like wet laundry headed for the spin cycle. Her short dark hair was kinky-limp and her blue "Phil's Tackle" T-shirt stuck to her back.

"You're a mess," said Gloria as Kate scrunched down the gravel path and flopped onto the hot deck.

"Yeeoow!" Kate leapt back up. The weathered boards were hot as a dashboard, even through her shorts. Gloria, who had just come out the screen door, went back inside and returned holding two beach towels with "Denver Broncos" in giant letters. Gloria was wearing khaki shorts and a bathing suit top. She spread the towels on the deck and stretched out facedown on one of them. Reaching around, she undid the catch of her suit. The straps hung down on either side like colorful little banners.

"My friends will razz me if I come home without a California tan. Could you put some of that lotion on my back?"

"Sure." Kate's hands were already sweaty with the heat and the bottle almost slithered out of her grasp. Kneeling on the deck, she squirted goop into her hand and started working it into Gloria's back and shoulders. The lotion was slippery under her fingers as she slid her hands down Gloria's back and then massaged up and down along the vertebrae. Gloria's shoulders relaxed and she sighed deeply as Kate worked the muscles around her neck and collarbones. She seemed to be melting into the deck. Kate's breathing fell into a rhythm. She slid her hands down to Gloria's waist and up to her shoulders. Down to her waist, and up to the nape of her neck.

"Kate," Gloria said softly after a few minutes, "you'd better stop."

Kate lay down on the other towel and stared up at the cloudless sky. She turned toward Gloria, who gazed at her for a few seconds, then smiled and closed her eyes. Kate shaded her eyes with one arm and drifted into a haze of heat and unfocused desire.

She recalled an afternoon last November when her school played hockey against Santa Rosa High on the field in the flats by Fife Creek, and the sky had opened up and dumped gallons of rain on them, but no one wanted to stop because they were in the last five minutes of the game. The field turned to mud, and they slipped on the boggy grass trying to catch the ball on their hockey sticks. No one could tell the white uniforms from the gold because everyone was mud brown and laughing as they slid around on the mucky field. She had walked home in the rain, wet and laughing, feeling her skin tingle beneath the soaked whites, and the feeling inside her now, though the day was hot and dry, was the same feeling.

Two days later, Gloria arranged to pick up Kate on the corner of Armstrong Woods Road. "I could have borrowed Uncle Phil's VW," Kate protested, climbing into the Ford. Skipper was on the truck bed, fogging the back window of the cab with enthusiasm as they headed west into the sun of late afternoon.

"There's a problem with the truck," Gloria said.

"It sounds okay—for an ancient truck," Kate said, wondering about the suspension after decades of potholes.

"The engine isn't the problem," Gloria said. "Carrie left me this truck. I can't stash it in the glove compartment of the Volvo when I drive home, and I can't see selling it to strangers. You're going to have to take it."

As they drove down River Road, Kate ran through a catalogue of possible futures. She was a successful landscaper hauling potted maples to distant estates, a carpenter with a truck full of tools, a photographer who, Ansel Adams-fashion, cruised the backroads in search of the perfect shot.

Gloria pulled into the drive, set the brake, and waved Kate out of the truck when she tried to say thanks.

"Listen," Gloria said, "I want to just be here alone a little while I say goodbye to the place. Why don't you take the Nikon and snap some scenes you think I should remember. I'll develop the film when I get home."

Kate looped the camera strap over her shoulder and trudged up the driveway, her sneakers making little craters in the gravel. She followed a deer path through the lupine to a cypress near the top of the ridge. Kate leaned against the trunk of the tree and pointed the lens at the post office by the dock across the river. The postmaster, Pauli Taglietto, would lock up the post office soon. He'd unclip the flag, fold it up and drive up the hill to his A-frame. He always took the flag with him and left it on the seat of his truck, to keep an eye on it, as if thieves would break in during the night and make off with his flag along with stamps and petty cash. Kate didn't think Gloria would care about Pauli and his flag, but she took a shot of the whole scene—the dock, the post office, and the gas station where the tourists stopped with their heavy station wagons to fill up before tackling the coast road to Mendocino.

As if on cue, an osprey grappling with a silver fish landed in another cypress fifty feet down the slope. Kate noiselessly rested the end of the lens on her drawn-up knees and used the zoom to draw him in. He held the fish against the branch with one talon and tugged at the flesh with his hooked beak as Kate took four exposures.

Down the hill, Gloria lowered the last box into the Volvo and slammed the trunk. Then she flopped into the deck chair, propping her heels on the railing. Kate, sitting in the dark under the tree, swung the camera toward her and zoomed in.

The day was hot and Gloria, dressed simply in white T-shirt and cutoff jeans, was breathing heavily from carrying the boxes. As Kate watched, Gloria's breathing evened out to a light movement under her shirt. Her eyes closed. Through the lens Kate studied Gloria's legs—the way sculpted muscles lay in repose from ankle to thigh, the way her hips relaxed, molded in the canvas chair. She had tucked one hand into a jeans pocket; the other arm hung loose over the side of the chair. Her fingertips touched the rim of a teacup left on the deck.

Whatever grief had lodged with Gloria, Kate thought, it hadn't made a permanent home. Gloria's features had been blurred by sadness but now, with a clarity enhanced by the camera, Kate saw a peacefulness there. She turned the lens until her friend came perfectly into focus, and took the shot.

Her Last Dog

Barbara L. Baer

In the photograph, my pregnant mother is kneeling on the gravel path with her hand on the head of Kip, a high-strung, yappy cocker spaniel who will be the cause of my premature birth some hours later. My mother stepped into the middle of a fight Kip picked with a chow. She managed to pull the dogs apart but went into labor that night. I was only eight months along, small and red, squawking like a chicken, not a pretty baby but fully ready, she always told me, to take on the big world as Kip had done.

Now I see another picture taken three years later and similarly posed, of my mother with another beloved dog, this one a young and gentle spaniel named Bart who would grow up with me. My mother is smiling, happy because I'm thriving and she is a few months pregnant with my younger brother. Her shining black hair curls closely against her head like a cap. Her dress is a light print with a wide, white collar, shoulder pads, and short sleeves that show her robust arms resting on Bart's coat. The picture shifts focus and I see myself sitting beside her, but this cannot be because in the picture she is forty and so am I, which, even as I dream, I know is impossible. My eyes brim over with tears so that I feel them on my cheeks without waking up. The last hours before my flight to New Zealand, I ran around doing things that wasted time I could have sat talking with her. I tried to reach her Christmas day but my call never got through. *It's all right,* she says. Those are her only words, but she communicates to me a feeling that everything is fine.

I'm forced from the cocoon of my dream by a crying sound at the door. Damn, it's her last dog, Cleo, whom I rescued from my brother a few weeks ago because he couldn't take care of himself, much less a dog, though he had wanted Cleo to remind him of our mother. Cleo has gained back most of the weight she lost while he kept her outdoors in a yard full of refuse and syringes, but she's not happy just being fed and safe. Even in warm weather, she wants to sleep near someone. Despite baths and sprays, she scratches and she smells. I, too, put her out, an exile she takes personally even though our own dogs sleep with her.

For at least ten years, Cleo never strayed more than a few feet from my mother. She curled up in the kitchen while my mother cooked, lay by her chair as she read, kept a vigil beside her bed, alert to every movement. She probably took in my mother's sadness about my father who was losing his mind to dementia, and all her worries over my brother's addiction and reckless life. But even at the worst of times, my mother lived hoping for the best, lived the day-to-day, lived without fear. She slept with her door wide open to accommodate Cleo, who barked at every creature in the fields and flung herself between my mother and shadows. Cleo lay low when my brother was sneaking into my mother's room and stealing money from her purse. My mother went to the bank every few days to have the cash on hand because the people my brother owed were not the kind to wait.

Cleo's ears are outsized like a coyote's and catch every sound. They poke out horizontally from her head like tawny tulips or organic scanners. Even now in her mourning, her sense of play comes through those huge ears—she cocks one, nods, tosses her head to tell you to come, follow her. She slaps the floor with her paw to signal she wants one of our dogs or cats to chase her. I've noticed that she only shows her comic side to animals, as if people were a more serious matter. She's become our fiercest barker when a person or animal approaches, but within minutes, her tawny tail wags, because she's friendly as well as vigilant.

Cleo is maternal and licks our cats until they're sticky. We knew that she had at least one litter before my mother found her on the side of a road, her nipples swollen from recent birth. She was terrified of popping sounds. We never knew whether they reminded her of guns or whips. Whatever Cleo had suffered in her earliest days, to become my mother's companion was to be reborn into heaven on earth. She ate bits of meat and gravy stirred warm into her kibble. Every trip to the store, Cleo, like all her predecessors, sat proudly in the back seat, shedding and lending a doggy smell to the car. My mother was indifferent to hairs on her clothes or furniture. She put animals' pleasures on a par with humans' and always saved the best part of her sugar cone, the sweet, toffee-like end, for Cleo who waited patiently.

My mother suffered a cerebral hemorrhage the morning after I failed to reach her from New Zealand to wish her Merry Christmas. I know she died the way she wanted to, no extraordinary means employed, no lingering in an invalid's helpless half-life, but she was gone so suddenly that I never had a chance to say good-by. At least my brother was with her. He had brought her morning coffee and was beside her when she had the stroke. He called 911 but did not ride in the ambulance with her. Two days earlier, he had discharged himself from the hospital against doctors' orders with a wound still oozing; he was wrecked, disoriented, and more than anything, afraid that he'd have to manage alone without his drugs.

We warm-blooded beings are programmed to go on, to eat, to seek shelter and affection. Cleo still waits for food in her dish, wants to be patted, cries to be let into the house. My son doesn't like her, doesn't want an older, smelly, scratching dog when we already have two nice young ones of our own. When the vet checked Cleo, he said she was malnourished and flea-ridden—from the period with my brother, who since my mother's death does not bathe or feed himself—but that otherwise she appeared healthy. I give her buffered aspirin for her arthritic hind legs. For my brother, the painkillers and pain-avoiders have over the years become drugs of a much more dangerous sort. I can't deal with his addiction, can't care for him as well as care for my own family, while

I can keep Cleo as a partial fulfillment of what I owe my mother.

My mother didn't believe in a heaven, but she felt the spirit of every creature alive continued in some way, somewhere, and on rare occasions might contact us, as she was sure her own mother had done.

Save Rolley, my mother heard her mother say as clearly as if she'd been standing beside her, as clearly as I heard her speak to me before Cleo started crying. Rolley was a thoroughbred, a failed racehorse my grandfather bought in a mad moment to give his wife. When Rolley proved a dud on the track, my grandfather had him sold to be used at stud. All of this happened long before I was born, before my mother married, but it was a story I loved to hear.

In the days that followed her dream, my mother searched in all the southern California stud farms and stables. She followed leads from trainers and jockeys. Finally, she found Rolley in a dark stall, covered with festering wounds, his hindquarters damaged from being over-used for breeding. The grooms prodded him with a pitchfork, called him vicious and crazy, a killer-horse. My mother bought back Rolley on the spot, but not before she pinned the horse's owner to the wall with the pitchfork and told him she'd like to do to him what he'd done to Rolley. My mother stood slightly over five feet, was kindness itself except when she was fighting injustice to children or cruelty to animals. I can see her backing a big man to the wall, holding those tines against his throat and scaring him nearly to death before she put the tool down and walked out.

As a child, I never tired of hearing what happened after that. More searching turned up the horse's former trainer who worked in a girls' boarding school. My mother gave Rolley to the school, where he became the darling of the little girls who wove flowers in his mane and tail and rode him around the ring, three or four at a time, facing forward, facing back. He never did one mean or dangerous thing and finally died of old age.

Though it's August, the fog is rolling in from the coast and the night is chilly. I see billows outside the window. I get up, find my robe, slip out the door. There's Cleo, wagging her tail, whimpering with eagerness to communicate who-knows-what sounds and spirits. Did my mother come to visit her as well? My mother loved us all equally, not the same, but equal to what we needed. She may have come to Cleo as well as to me. All at once I want to love Cleo as my mother did, to see her as my mother saw her, as a being with a full heart and soul.

My mother didn't tell me how I should live my life. She did good by instinct rather than from weighing evidence. She tried to save my father's dignity to the last, tried to save my brother from drugs and despair, and though she couldn't change the outcome of their lives, she never gave them up or loved them less. I take Cleo's head in my lap, feel her big ears. Inside they're warm, outside they're cold. She snuggles close, stretching her vertebrae the way dogs do when they're utterly happy to be stroked. Cleo is willing to love again, not as she loved before, but to love.

I'll try to love Cleo better, if you'll come to me again, I say to my mother, bargaining. I don't know anymore than Cleo does what I'm going to do for the rest of my life without you. Only come to me once again. I have such desire to see you.

ORDER FORM

Floreant Press
Barbara L. Baer
6195 Anderson Road
Forestville, CA 95436
Telephone (707) 887-7868

Please send me ______ copies of
Cartwheels on the Faultline at $12.50 each.

Please include $2.00 shipping and handling for the first copy and $1 for each additional copy.
Californians: Please add 7.5 percent sales tax.

Name ____

Address ______________________________________

________________________________ Zip __________